MW00462883

Script Fonts

Script Fonts

Geum-Hee Hong

Laurence King Publishing

Contents

Foreword

Script fonts and their cousins have taken foundries' bestseller lists by storm, bringing personality and authenticity to printed material of all kinds, from business cards to flyers and packaging to adverts. They include fonts that mimic handwriting – using an array of different letterforms – to classic English scripts in the manner of eighteenth-century copperplate engravings, and everything in between. Whether they suggest a pen or brush, graffiti or punk, incorporate naïve, childish curlicues or clever typographical technology – as in the ubiquitous 'Zapfino' – these retro fonts evoke another age.

So what could be more natural than to write a book about the phenomenon of script type? Not a straightforward collection – much less one that aspired to be exhaustive, as wonderful new fonts are being created all the time – but a guide to the script-font jungle, an attempt to sort and classify them according to both stylistic era and the tools whose distinctive appearance they borrow. In collaboration with Korean expert Geum-Hee Hong, we embarked on our search, deliberately selecting not only the best and most beautiful examples of handwriting, but also curiosities like the digitized handwriting of famous presidents or Paul Cézanne. If the more than 300 script fonts presented here in all their variety inspire you to use them, you can also find information on suppliers and designers, as well as a CD with 122 free fonts you can try out to get you started.

We recommend you think carefully about whether a particular font suits your requirements and creative needs. Script fonts, in particular, because they simulate having been written in a single stroke, hinge on perfectly adjusted transitions between the letters. In order to illustrate this more clearly, we have included – alongside representative character sets – treasure-map clues, shopping lists and recipes that showcase the style of the script across a small block of text. We always list a point size, since script fonts, with a few exceptions, mostly have unusually large ascenders and descenders!

Books like *Script Fonts* are only made possible through the support of foundries and type designers across the world. We want to thank everybody who gave us typefaces, visual material, permissions and advice. We are grateful for the varied enthusiasm and interest of all those who lent a hand along the way, contributing to and supporting this project. Particular thanks are due to Geum-Hee Hong. Let yourself be carried away by her passion for hand-lettering!

Karin and Bertram Schmidt-Friderichs
Mainz, Summer 2010

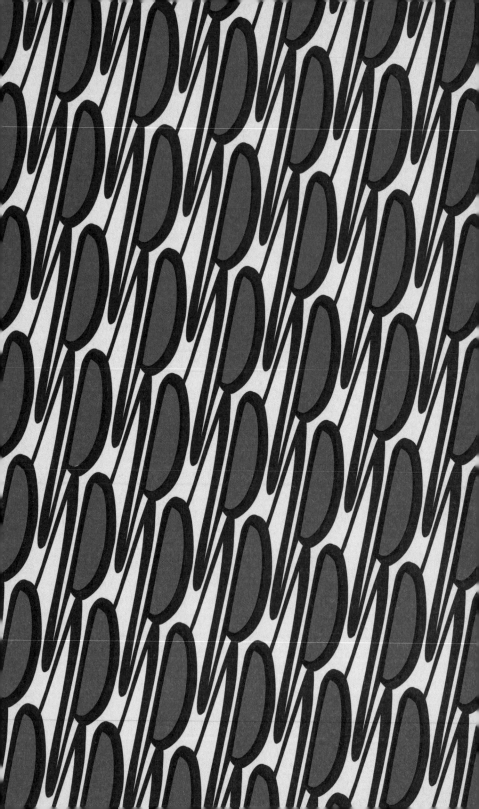

Handwriting

Spontaneous and Personal

All scripts are ultimately based on handwriting. Printed handwriting is essentially anachronistic, though, conversely, writers of official documents once aspired to 'write like print' – in other words, extreme regularity and evenness were considered ideal. Today it is possible to have your own handwriting digitized, complete with randomly scattered alternative letterforms to lend the script extra authenticity. As one might expect, there is also a whole range of fonts modelled on famous people's handwriting, from George Washington to Picasso to pirates' scrawls!

Handwriting represents authenticity and sincerity, exclusivity and spontaneity, individuality and personal expression. It has evoked these qualities for centuries, whether in your great-grandmother's secret recipe or used to quote the founder of a company, for a brilliant, off-the-cuff first draft or to give a testimonial an individual touch. It can appear young or old, feminine or masculine. And in graphic design, handwriting offers a welcome respite from the computerized perfection of graphics programs!

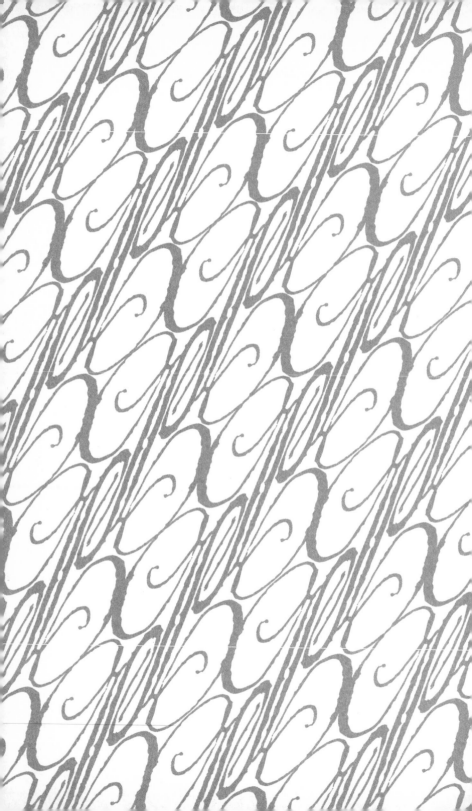

ABCDEFGHIJKLMN
OPQRSTUVWXYZ

abcdefghijklmnopqrstuvwxyzäöüß

† ⚶ $ % @ & ?!..,:; ❋

1234567890

29 Point

Forsaking monastic tradition, twelve jovial friars gave up their
vocation for a questionable existence on the flying trapeze.

14/30 Point

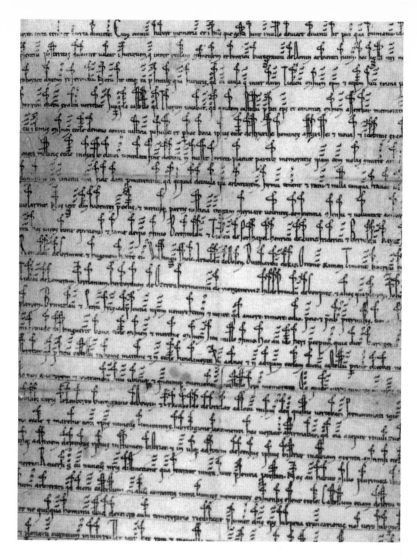

German official document, 1206

VESPASIANO · AMPHYARE · MINORITANO ·

Qq ſs ſ tſ f fu x y ß &

GRandißimo dileto guſtano le humane menti benignißimo lettore nella dolce rimé=
branza delli ſanti precem de antichi Philoſophi, et delli predariſſimi fani de indut, et
fortiſſimi Imperatori, Onde il gran Stupore di Natura et priape di Peripatetiq, in=
ſegnaua ad Aleß Maced. uolgere e riuolgere gli annali della antichità da quali ſé=
pre hauerià trouato materià di paſcer l'intelleto, e riuſtire illuſtre. Que benefìcio
in noi deriua p la ſola mercede delli ſacrati augelli dello antico Pallamede li gli à
mal grado del tempo ne liberano dalla obliuione di coſe tanto degne et eccellenti.

Al ſuo Giouan Battiſta Ciardi. A a b c d e f f g h ij k l m n o p

Idem Ar Veſpaſian

Deſiderando io ſommamente humaniſſ lettore dimoſtrare al mondo quanto ſ
bontà diuina in me ſi troui Eccellente latte de lo ſcriuere uarie, et diuerſe
maniere di ſlette, ne potendo preſentialmente eſſere in ſiu d'un luogo mj
ſono Intertenuto in queſto picciolo mondo che coſi ſj puo chiamare la Inclita
et magnifica Città di Venetia. Oue con ogni ſtudio, et Diligenza mj ſono
poſto ad ordinare la fabrica di mio libretto di lettra baſtarda, à comune
Vtilitade de amatorj di virtù et particulare ſodisfattice de gli amig. etc.

Amphyareus ſcribeba.

From the writing manual of Vespasiano
Amphiareo, Venice, 1554

Handwriting

18

A B C D E F G
H I J K L M N
O P Q R S T U
V W X Y Z

abcdefghijklmnopqrstu
vwxyzäöüß$%&@?!.,:;*
1234567890

42 Point

Forsaking monastic tradition, twelve jovial friars gave up their vocation for a questionable existence on the flying trapeze.

18/22 Point

Handwriting

19

ABCDEF
GHIJKLMN
OPQRSTU
VWXYZ

abcdefghijklmnopqrstuvwxyzäöüß

$%&@?!.,:;* 1234567890

30 Point

Forsaking monastic tradition, twelve jovial friars gave up their

vocation for a questionable existence on the flying trapeze.

15/35 Point

A B C D E F G
H I J K L M N
O P Q R S T U
V W X Y Z

abcdefghijklmnopqrstuvwxyz

äöüß $%&@?!.,:;*

1234567890

55 Point

Forsaking monastic tradition, twelve jovial friars gave up their vocation for a questionable existence on the flying trapeze.

26/24 Point

Handwriting

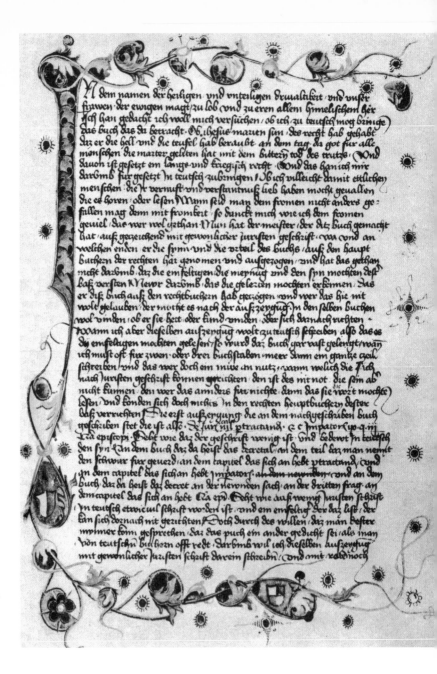

In dem namen der heiligen vnd vnteiligen drivaltikeit vnd vnsir
frawen der ewigen magt/zu lob vnd zu eren allem himelischem hêr
Ich han gedacht ich woll mich versüchen / ob ich zu teutsch mocht bringe
das buch das da betracht. Ob ihesus marien sun des recht hab gehabt
daz er die hell vnd die teufel hab beraubt an dem tag da got fur alle
menschen die marter geliten hat mit dem bittery tod des trutze Vnd
dauon ist gesetzt em lange vnd kriegisch recht Vnd das han ich mir
darvmb fur gesetzt In teutsch zubringen Ob euch villeicht damit ettlichen
menschen die ir vernuft vnd verstantnuß lieb haben mocht geuallen
die es horen oder lesen Wann seid man dem fromen nicht anders ge-
fallen mag dann mit fromkeit / so dunckt mich wie ich dem fromen
geuiel das wer wol gethan Nun hat der meister der diz buch gemacht
hat auß gezeichend mit gewonlicher iuristen geschrift an vond an
welchen enden er die sinn vnd die vrteil des buchs / auß den haupt
buchern der rechten hat genomen vnd aufgezogen vnd hat das gethan
mehe darvmb daz die em festigten die meynüg vnd den syn mochten deß
baß verften Newor darvmb das die geleten mochten erkennen das
er diß buch auß den rechtbuchern hab gezogen vnd wer das hie mit
wolt gelauben / so mocht es nach der auß zeygnüg In den selben buchen
wol vinden ob er sie hett oder kund vinden der sich darnach richten
Wann ich aber dieselben auszeygnüg wolt zuteutsch schreiben also das es
die emfeltigen mochten gelesen so wurd das buch gar vast gelengt wan
ich muft oft fur zwen oder drei buchstaben meer dann em gantze teil
schreiben vnd das wer doch em miue an nutz wann welich die sich
nach iuristen geschrift konnen gerichten den ist des mit not die sinn ab
nicht kumen den wer das anders fur nichte dann das sie woit mochte
lesen vnd konden sich doch nichts In den rechten heuptbuchern dester
baß verrichten Die erst aufsergunge die an dem nachgeschriben buch
geschriben stet die ist also De iure vil ptractand. e c Impator. yo q. iij
Ixa episcopi Seht wie daz der geschrift wenig ist vnd selbewt In teutsch
den syn In dem buch daz da heist das decretal an dem teil letz man nemt
den schwour fur geuerd an dem capitel das sich an hebt ptractand vnd
yn dem capitel das sich an hebt Impator an dem nevnden vnd an dem
buch daz da heist daz decret an der nevonden sach an der dritten frag an
dem capitel das sich an hebt La epi Seht wie auß wenig haisten schrift
In teutsch etwa vil schrift worden ist vnd em emfeltig der daz lift der
kan sich darnach mit gerichten Doch durch des willen diz man dester
wminer kom gespreechen daz das puch em ander gedicht sei also man
von teutschn buchern offt redt darvmb wil ich dieselben auszeygnüg
mit gewonlicher iuristen schrift darein schreiben Vnd mit reden noch

Pia Frauss, 2007 | pia-frauss.de | CD

28 Point

Forsaking monastic tradition, twelve
jovial friars gave up their vocation for
a questionable existence on the wing

13/23 Point

Handwriting

Peter Wiegel, 2009 | peter-wiegel.de | CD

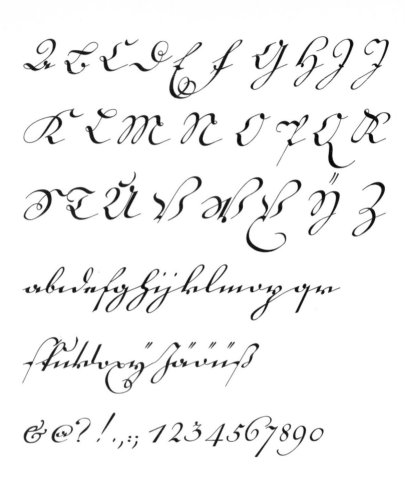

36 Point

15/25 Point

Wer in der Jugend hat besucht die Schreibe-
Schuel, wer hat auch allemahl sein Brod und
Brod gewinnen, kann kann Schreiben, Auch
wer im Latein, will Sie kauft richten Krieg auch
kindten Hier im Rhein. Drum wer was gewin-
lichs verstehet, den hält man werth, den Unge-
schickten aber gar Niemand begehret.

am bm cm dm em fm ffm ffm gm hm
im km ckm lm llm mm nm om pm qm
rm em sm fm ßm ftm tm ttm um vm
wm xm ym zm zm

24 Point

Forsaking monastic tradition, twelve jovial friars gave up their vocation for a questionable existence on the flying trapeze.

12/24 Point

Stefan Kroemer, 2006 | myfonts.com

ABCDEFGHI
JKLMNOPQR
STUVWXYZ

abcdefghijklmn
opqrstuvwxyzäöüß
§%e$?!.,:;✶

1234567890

66 Point

Forsaking monastic tradition, twelve jovial
friars gave up their vocation for a questionable
existence on the flying trapeze.

28/24 Point

Handwriting

*A B C D E F G H
I J K L M N O P Q
R S T U V W X Y Z*

*abcdefghijklmn
opqrstuvwxyzäöüß*

*& § @ $? ! . , : ; ***

1 2 3 4 5 6 7 8 9 0

40 Point

---

*Forsaking monastic tradition, twelve
jovial friars gave up their vocation for a
questionable existence on the flying trapeze.*

18/24 Point

Handwriting

Eine Kinderstube [A Nursery], c. 1785

Pia Frauss, 2007 | pia-frauss.de | CD

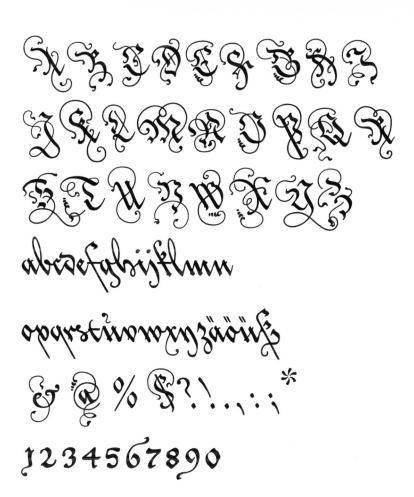

29 Point

Forsaking monastic tradition, twelve jovial
friars gave up their vocation for a questionable
existence on the flying trapeze.

15/22 Point

Handwriting

Corradine Fonts–Manuel Eduardo Corradine, 2008 | myfonts.com

ABCDEFGHIJ
KLMNOPQR
STUVWXYZ
abcdefghijklmn
opqrstuvwxyzäöüß
§$%&,@?!.,:;*
1234567890

54 Point

Forsaking monastic tradition, twelve jovial
friars gave up their vocation for a questionable
existence on the flying trapeze.

22/24 Point

ABCDEFGHIJ
KLMNOPQR
STUVWXYZ
abcdefghijklmnopqrstuvw
xyzäöüß $%&@?!.,:;*
1234567890

57 Point

Forsaking monastic tradition, twelve jovial friars
gave up their vocation for a questionable existence on
the flying trapeze.

24/24 Point

Handwriting

33

Gli huomini vanno allo studio per sapersi preualere
tra gli huomini maluagi et disordinati L'imparare
scienza ad altro non gioua Che ad emendare la vita
et sapere raffrenare la lingua. b, g, x, y.

Ogni huomo che opera male ha in odio la luce accioche l'opere
sue maligne non sieno manifeste: Ma colui che segue la
uerita uiena alla luce accioche l'opere sue sieno chiare,
pche le sono fatte in Dio. b, d, g, v, x, y, y, z.

L'inuidia è passion diabolica et infermita che non si puo
guarire. Qualunque proua dolor nel capo scuopre al
medico la sua indispositione: ma l'inuidioso come dira
il suo male?

From the writing manual *Les escritures
financière, et italienne - bastarde dans leur
naturel,* Par Louis Barbedor, Paris 1647

Pia Frauss, 2007 | pia-frauss.de | CD

24 Point

Forsaking monastic tradition, twelve jovial friars gave up their vocation for a questionable existence on the flying trapeze.

12/25 Point

A B C D E F

G H I J K L M N

O P Q R S T

U V W X Y Z

abcdefghijklmnopqrstuvw

xyzäöüſſ§%&@?!.,:;

1234567890

42 Point

Forsaking monastic tradition, twelve jovial friars gave up their vocation for a questionable existence on the flying trapeze.

20/23 Point

The Declaration of Independence, by Thomas Jefferson.
A printing from 1823

A B C D E F G
H I J K L M
N O P Q R S
T U V W X Y Z

abcdefghijklmnopq
rstuvwxyzäöüß

*& § @ % $? ! . , : ; ` ***

1 2 3 4 5 6 7 8 9 0

43 Point

Forsaking monastic tradition, twelve jovial
friars gave up their vocation for a questionable
existence on the flying trapeze.

23/25 Point

A B C D E F G H I J
K L M N O P Q R
S T U V W X Y Z

abcdefghijklmnopqrstuvw
xyzäöüß&@%$?!.,:; *
1234567890

45 Point

Forsaking monastic tradition, twelve jovial friars
gave up their vocation for a questionable existence on
the flying trapeze.

20/25 Point

Handwriting

39

landed on its four legs, I mean the four wheels
the driver holding on to the reins, soon stoped
the fiery steeds, and after a proper flagellation
for their lawless conduct, he attempted the Bridge
a second time & crossed without dificulty. The
passengers resumed their seats, and I was rather
pleased than otherwise with the adventure, be
cause it made the driver, in resentment, double
the speed of his common gait, and dash along
at the comfortable & cheering rate of 6 mile an
hour. The generous passenger who felt alarmed at
my setuation, ran to the coach as she slow
cleared the Bridge to awaken me, beleiving me
to be a sleep, and earnestly entreated me to make
my escape out of the window before the horses
should down the Banks. In this he
evinced a good heart, a benevolent principle, &
which more excites my admiration and affect
than personal accomplishments or intellectual
attainments. The road to Montgomery was in
good order; the tavern at which we stoped was
of the first rate, and every thing during my
abidance there contributed to make the delay
rather acceptable than irksome. Between Columb
& Montgomery I met with but little that excited reflection or worthy of divercy

The reader may possibly desire
to learn something about this Town as it is one of

Mirabeau B. Lamar, travel journal,
by Mirabeau Buonaparte Lamar, 1835
(June to October, 1835)

Three Islands Press, 2002, 2006 | oldfonts.com

A B C D E F G H

I J K L M N O P Q

R S T U V W X Y Z

a b c d e f g h i j k l m n

o p q r s t u v w x y z

ä ö ü ß ff ♦ $ % & &

? ! . , : ; * ——

1 2 3 4 5 6 7 8 9 0

31 Point

Forsaking monastic tradition, twelve
jovial friars gave up their vocation for a
questionable existence on the flying trapeze.

11/25 Point

Handwriting

41

ABCDEFGH

IJKLMNOPQ

RSTUVWXYZ

abcdefghijklmn

opqrstuvwxyzäöüß

§$%&()@.?!.,:;*

1234567890

37 Point

Forsaking monastic tradition, twelve jovial
friars gave up their vocation for a questionable
existence on the flying trapeze.

16/23 Point

ABCDEFGH

IJKLMNOPQ

RSTUVWXYZ

abcdefghijklmn

opqrstuvwxyz

äöüß§$%&@?!.,:;*

1234567890

38 Point

Forsaking monastic tradition, twelve
jovial friars gave up their vocation for a
questionable existence on the flying trapeze.

14/25 Point

Handwriting

43

A B C D E F G H I
J K L M N O P Q R
S T U V W X Y Z
abcdefghijklmn
opqrstuvwx yzäöüß
$ %@ ? ! . , : ; *
1 2 3 4 5 6 7 8 9 0

52 Point

Forsaking monastic tradition, twelve
jovial friars gave up their vocation for
a questionable existence on the flying trapeze.

21/24 Point

Handwriting

ABCDEFGHIJ
KLMNOPQR
STUVWXYZ
abcdefghijklmn
opqrstuvwxyzäöüß
$%&@?!.,:;*
1234567890

56 Point

Forsaking monastic tradition, twelve jovial friars
gave up their vocation for a questionable existence
on the flying trapeze.

22/24 Point

Poster, Volker Pfüller, 2004

ABCDEFGH
IJKLMNOPQ
RSTUVWXYZ

abcdefghijklmnopqr
stuvwxyzäöüß

$%&@?!.,:; *

1234567890

33 Point

_____

Forsaking monastic tradition, twelve jovial friars
gave up their vocation for a questionable existence
on the flying trapeze.

15/23 Point

Handwriting

47

ABCDEFGH
IJKLMNOPQ
RSTUVWXYZ
abcdefghijklmn
opqrstuvwxyzäöüß
§$&@!#.,;;*
1234567890

46 Point

Forsaking monastic tradition, twelve
jovial friars gave up their vocation for a
questionable existence on the flying trapeze.

18/21 Point

nemen moet - Dit is zoowat 't effect van den knotwil
maar in de aquarel zelf is geen zwart dan in gebroken toestand.

vaar op dit schetsje het zwart 't donkerst is zitten de grootste
kracten in de aquarel. — donkergroen bruin
raauw. Nu adieu, en geloof me dat sommylen
ik er hartelyk om lach dat de lui my flu eigentlyk
nets anders ben dan een vriend van de natuur van
ludre, van werk — ook van menschen vooral / verder
an diverse kwaadaardigheden en absurditeiten waaraan
een haar op myn hoofd denkt. Enfin — tot ziens
met een handdruk   h. t.   Vincent

A letter by Vincent van Gogh, July 1882

Excerpt from a letter by Paul Cézanne
to Emile Zola, 30 June 1866

A B C D E F G H I J

K L M N O P Q

R S T U V W X Y Z

a b c d e f g h i j k l m n

o p q r s t u v w x y z ä ä ü ß t

*$ % & @ ? ! . , ; : * Cezanne*

1 2 3 4 5 6 7 8 9 0

36 Point

---

*Forsaking monastic tradition, twelve jovial friars
gave up their vocation for a questionable existence on
the flying trapeze.*

16/25 Point

ABCDEFGH
IJKLMNOPQR
STUVWXYZ

abcdefghijklmn

opqrstuvwxyzäöüß

&%§?!.,:; *

1234567890

49 Point

Forsaking monastic tradition, twelve jovial friars
gave up their vocation for a questionable existence
on the flying trapeze.

19/23 Point

vous verrai. Chaque jour
plus difficille et du
calme ou? — Je suis
en train de faire un
home avec une petite
fille ils porten des
fleur dan un panier
à coté de eux deux
voulufs et du bles
quelque chose comme ça

Mes meilleures
souvenirs à votre sœur
et à vous de votre ami
Picasso

A letter to Leo and Gertrude Stein,
Pablo Picasso, Paris, 1906

A B C D E F G H
I J K L M N O P Q
R S T U V W X Y Z
a b c d e f g h i j k l m n
o p q r s t u v w x y z ä ö ü ß
† § % & @ ? ! . , : ; *
1 2 3 4 5 6 7 8 9 0

42 Point

Forsaking monastic tradition, twelve
jovial friars gave up their vocation for a
questionable existence on the flying trapeze.

16/25 Point

Handwriting

Viktor Solt, 1998 | linotype.com

A B C D E F G H I J

K L L M N O P Q R

S T U V W X Y Z

a b c d e f g h i j k l m n

o p q r s t u v w x y z ä ö ü ß

*$ % § @ & ? ! . , . ; ***

1 2 3 4 5 6 7 8 9 0

39 Point

Forsaking monastic tradition, twelve jovial friars gave up their vocation for a questionable existence on the flying trapeze.

20/25 Point

other put-offs. I must come to you
... if it be possible, for on that day
...don for a week or two with your ...
expected here on Sunday. If Monday
... appear too dirty for walking, & Mr B
so kind as to come & fetch me ...
... of the morn) with you, I
... obliged to him. Cassy might
... & your Aunt Cassandra will
opportunity. —
... sends her Love & Thanks for your
very happy to hear the contents of your
... she will send the Strawberry roots
... as early next week as the ...
allow her to take them up. —

Yours very affec:ly
my dear Anna
          J. Austen

Excerpt from a letter by Jane Austen,
29 September 1815

ABCDEFGHIJ
KLMNOPQR
STUVWXYZ

abcdefghijklmnopq
rstuvwxyzäöüß
%&@?!.,;:* the

1234567890

30 Point

Forsaking monastic tradition, twelve
jovial friars gave up their vocation for a
questionable existence on the flying trapeze.

13/25 Point

Handwriting

A B C D E F G
H I J K L M
N O P Q R S T U
V W X Y Z
a b c d e f g h i j k l m n
o p q r s t u v w x y z
*ä ö ü ß & $ % @ ? ! . , : ; ***
1 2 3 4 5 6 7 8 9 0

33 Point

Forsaking monastic tradition, twelve jovial friars gave up their vocation for a questionable existence on the flying trapeze.

11/25 Point

James West, 1993 | myfonts.com

A B C D E F G
H I J K L M
N O P Q R S T
U V W X Y Z
a b c d e f g h i j k l m n
o p q r s t u v w x y z
ä ö ü ß $ % & @ ? ! . , : ; *
1 2 3 4 5 6 7 8 9 0

34 Point

Forsaking monastic tradition, twelve
jovial friars gave up their vocation for
a questionable existence on the flying trapeze.

12/25 Point

January 24, 1836

Dearest Gwendoline,

I cannot keep myself from writing any longer, although I have not had any response to either of my letters. How can I assure you that you have not been out of my thoughts even for one minute since I left you Sunday? You must know how effortlessy I love you & how much I would sacrifice if it were necessary to be married to live ever after with you.

Yours Lovingly,
Michael Hampshire

Dearest, Christina Torre, 2001

A B C D E F G H

I J K L M N O P Q

R S T U V W X Y Z

abcdefghijklmn

opqrstuvwxyzäöüß

$ % & @ . ? ! , . ; : *

1234567890

54 Point

Forsaking monastic tradition, twelve jovial
friars gave up their vocation for a questionable
existence on the flying trapeze.

28/25 Point

Handwriting

61

Kanna Aoki, 1995 | myfonts.com

A B C D E F G

H I J K L M N

O P Q R S T U

V W X Y Z

abcdefghijklmnopqrstuv

wxyzäöüß&¢$%?!.,:; *

1234567890

48 Point

Forsaking monastic tradition, twelve jovial friars gave up their vocation for a questionable existence on the flying trapeze.

24/25 Point

A B C D E F G
H I J K L M N
O P Q R S T U
V W X Y Z

abcdefghijklmnopqrstu

vwxyzäöüß§&@$?!.,:; *

1234567890

45 Point

Forsaking monastic tradition, twelve jovial friars gave up their vocation for a questionable existence on the flying trapeze.

22/25 Point

Handwriting

63

Three Islands Press, 2001, 2006 | oldfonts.com

A B C D E F G H I J

K L M N O P Q R

S T U V W X Y Z

a b c d e f g h i j k l m n

o p q r s t u v w x y z ä ö ü ß

$ % & @ ? ! . , : ; ⁎

1 2 3 4 5 6 7 8 9 0

45 Point

Forsaking monastic tradition, twelve
jovial friars gave up their vocation for a
questionable existence on the flying trapeze.

21/25 Point

Handwriting

64

ABCDEFGH
IJKLMNOPQ
RSTUVWXYZ
abcdefghijklmn
opqrstuvwxyzäöüß
$%&@?!.,;; *
1234567890

40 Point

Forsaking monastic tradition, twelve
jovial friars gave up their vocation for a
questionable existence on the flying trapeze.

15.5/25 Point

Handwriting

Poster, Jan Rajlich, 1988

Three Islands Press, 1996–98, 2006 | oldfonts.com

A B C D E F G H
I J K L M N O P Q
R S T U V W X Y Z

abcdefghijklmnopqrstu
vwxyzaoussttthie

$ % @ & . ? ! . , : ; ˮ
1 2 3 4 5 6 7 8 9 0

55 Point

Forsaking monastic tradition, twelve jovial
friars gave up their vocation for a questionable
existence on the flying trapeze.

26/25 Point

A B C D E F G
H I J K L M N
O P Q R S T U
V W X Y Z

abcdefghijklmnopqrstuvwxyz

äöüß §§$&@!#.,:; *

1 2 3 4 5 6 7 8 9 0

50 Point

Forsaking monastic tradition, twelve jovial
friars gave up their vocation for a questionable
existence on the flying trapeze.

36/25 Point

Handwriting

I like You
by Amy
Sedaris
hospitality
UNDER the
Influence

Book cover, Anne Twomey, 2006

Poster, Michael Bierut, 1999

Bright Ideas, 2008 | dafont.com | CD

A B C D E F G H

I J K L M N O P Q

R S T U V W X Y Z

abcdefghijklmnopqrstu

vwxyzäöüß&$?!.,:; *

1234567890

48 Point

Forsaking monastic tradition, twelve jovial
friars gave up their vocation for a questionable
existence on the flying trapeze.

22/25 Point

Erik van Blokland, Just van Rossum, 1990 | fontshop.com

ABCDEFGHIJKLMN
OPQRSTUVWXYZ
abcdefghijklmnop
qrstuvwxyzäöüß
§$%&@)?!.,.;*
1234567890

52 Point

Forsaking monastic tradition, twelve jovial friars
gave up their vocation for a questionable existence
on the flying trapeze.

18/25 Point

Handwriting

72

ABCDEFGH
IJKLMNOPQ
RSTUVWXYZ
abcdefghijklmn
opqrstuvwxyzäöüß
&§@%$?!.,.;*
1234567890

41 Point

Forsaking monastic tradition, twelve
jovial friars gave up their vocation for a
questionable existence on the flying trapeze.

18/25 Point

Erik van Blokland, Just van Rossum, 1990 | fontshop.com

ABCDEFGHIJ
KLMNOPQR
STUVWXYZ
abcdefghijklmn
opqrstuvwxyzäöüß
§ƒ%&@?!.,.:;*
1234567890

52 Point

Forsaking monastic tradition, twelve jovial
friars gave up their vocation for a questionable
existence on the flying trapeze.

18/22 Point

ABCDEFGHIJ
KLMNOPQR
STUVWXYZ
abcdefghijklmn
opqrstuvwxyzäöüß
§&%@$?!.,:;*
1234567890

52 Point

Forsaking monastic tradition, twelve
jovial friars gave up their vocation for a
questionable existence on the flying trapeze.

21/22 Point

Handwriting

ABCDEFGHIJ
KLMNOPQR
STUVWXYZ
abcdefghijklmn
opqrstuvwxyz
äöüß$&?!.,:;*
1234567890

40 Point

Forsaking monastic tradition, twelve
jovial friars gave up their vocation for a
questionable existence on the flying trapeze.

15/25 Point

Handwriting

Poster, Mats Gustavson, 1989

Italian and French Italics

The Forerunners of All Roman Cursives

Long before the advent of printing, scribes developed an alternative to the 'slow' hand typical of monastic writing: a cursive script where all the letterforms were differently shaped, largely to facilitate speed of execution, and where it was unnecessary to lift the pen from the page. Aldus Manutius used this typeface for his books, having it cut in lead; his work profoundly influenced almost all italic fonts to the present day.

Regional variants had always existed in handwriting, differing from writing master to writing master, and thus different italic scripts emerged in cultural centres like Florence, Rome or Venice, such as Cancellaresca romana or Cancellaresca formata.

Italics developed further in the eighteenth century, influenced by the style of writing used in copperplate engraving – the results can be seen in the next chapter. 'ITC Zapf Chancery' (page 96) and 'Zapfino' (page 101) are modern interpretations of these old broad-nib scripts.

In France there emerged a rounder, more ornate kind of handwriting. Examples include 'Civilite MJ' (page 130) and 'ITC Redonda' (page 129), which were written with the pen held at a steep angle.

A B C D E F G

H I J K L M N

O P Q R S T V

V W X Y Z

abcdefghijklmnopqrstuvwxyzäöüß

&§z$@?!.,:;*1234567890

42 Point

Forsaking monastic tradition, twelve jovial friars gave up their vocation for a questionable existence on the flying trapeze.

28/25 Point

Qualunque nelle virtuose attioni-
uassi il giorno auanzando in loro
tesoro pretiosiss.mo; et porge stupo

QVEMADMODVM desiderat ceruus ad fo
aquarum ita desiderat anima mea ad te De
Sitiuit anima mea ad DEVM Fontem v

Cancellaresca corrente, Cancellaresca formatella,
from a writing manual by Giovanni Francesco
Cresci, Rome, 1570

ABCDEFGHI
JKLMNOPQ
RSTUVWXYZ

abcdefghijklmnopqrstuvw

xyzäöüß&$%$@?!.,.:;*

1234567890

43 Point

Forsaking monastic tradition, twelve jovial friars
gave up their vocation for a questionable existence
on the flying trapeze.

21/25 Point

Italian and French Italics

ABCDEFGHI
JKLMNOPQR
STUVWXYZ

abcdefghijklmn
opqrstuvwxyzäöüß
&%$@?!.,.:;*
1234567890

42 Point

Forsaking monastic tradition, twelve jovial
friars gave up their vocation for a questionable
existence on the flying trapeze.

17/25 Point

Italian and French Italics

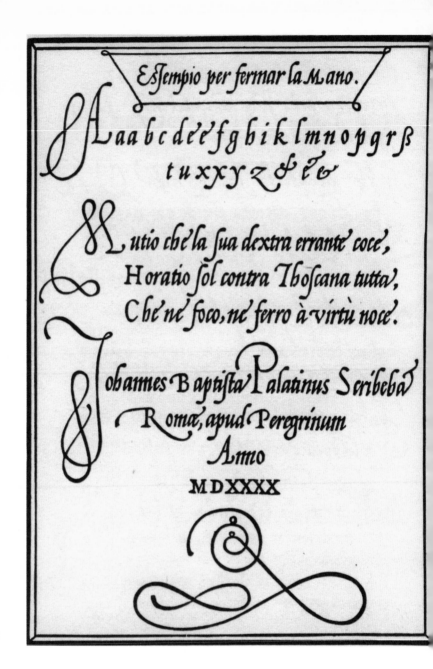

Essempio per fermar la Mano.

A a a b c d e e f g h i k l m n o p q r ß
t u x x y z & e &

Lutio che la sua dextra errante coce,
Horatio sol contra Thoscana tutta,
Che ne foco, ne ferro à virtù noce.

Johannes Baptista Palatinus Scribeba
Romæ, apud Peregrinum
Anno
MDXXXX

From a writing manual
by Johannes Baptista Palatinus (Palatino),
Rome, 1540

𝒜𝐵𝒞𝒟𝐸𝐹𝒢𝐻𝐼𝒥
𝒦�ℒ𝑀𝒩𝒪𝒫𝒬𝑅
𝒮𝒯𝒰𝒱𝒲𝒳𝒴𝒵

abcdefghijklmn

opqrstuvwxyzäöüß

℮ @ § $?! . , . ; * 𝕻𝕱

1234567890

31 Point

---

*Forsaking monastic tradition, twelve jovial friars
gave up their vocation for a questionable existence
on the flying trapeze.*

16/25 Point

Italian and French Italics

Gilles Le Corre, 2009 | gilleslecorre.com

A B C D E F G
H I J K L M
N O P Q R S T
U V W X Y Z

abcdefghijklmn
opqrstuvwxyzäöüß

§&%$?!,.:;*

1234567890

36 Point

Forsaking monastic tradition, twelve jovial friars
gave up their vocation for a questionable
existence on the flying trapeze.

15/25 Point

ABCDEFG

HIJKLM

NOPQRST

UVWXYZ

abcdefghijklmnopqrstuvwxyz

äöüß S & %$ @ ?!.,.; *

1234567890

45 Point

Forsaking monastic tradition, twelve jovial
friars gave up their vocation for a questionable
existence on the flying trapeze.

25/25 Point

Italian and French Italics

ABCDEFGHI
JKLMNOPQ
RSTUVWXYZ

abcdefghijklmn

opqrstuvwxyz

1234567890

46 Point

Forsaking monastic tradition, twelve jovial friars gave up their vocation for a questionable existence on the flying trapeze.

18/22 Point

Dollhouse

Suisse Miss

The Descent of God

Veganschnitzel

Symphony No.9

extra large

Gerschtöpenfrümflopen

MAN OR ASTROMAN?

Chancery titles

Ken Barber, 2009

Poster, Holger Matthies, 1993

A B C D E F G
H I J K L M N
O P Q R S T U
V W X Y Z

abcdefghijklmn

opqrstuvwxyzäöüß

&$?!.,:;1234567890

53 Point

Forsaking monastic tradition, twelve jovial friars
gave up their vocation for a questionable existence
on the flying trapeze.

23/25 Point

ABCDEFGHIJ
KLMNOPQR
STUVWXYZ
abcdefghijklmn
opqrstuvwxyzäöüß
&$%@?!.,:;*
1234567890

44 Point

Italian and French Italics

Forsaking monastic tradition, twelve jovial friars
gave up their vocation for a questionable existence
on the flying trapeze.

16/24 Point

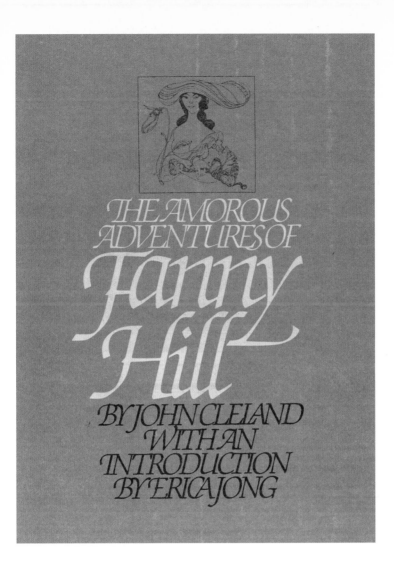

Book cover, Herb Lubalin, 1979

Catalogue, Anthony Deleo, Shane Keane, 2009

Demetrio E. Cabarga, Leslie Cabarga, 1982 | linotype.com

ABCDEFGH
IJKLMNOPQ
RSTUVWXYZ
abcdefghijklmn
opqrstuvwxyz
äöüß$&?!.,.;*
1234567890

41 Point

Forsaking monastic tradition, twelve
jovial friars gave up their vocation for a
questionable existence on the flying trapeze.

15/25 Point

Italian and French Italics

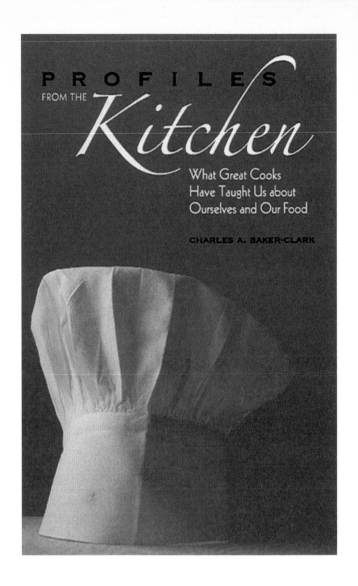

Book cover, The University Press of Kentucky, 2006

ABCDEFGH
IJKLMNOPQ
RSTUVWXYZ
abcdefghijklmn
opqrstuvwxyzäöüß
&$‰@?!.,:;*
1234567890

55 Point

*Forsaking monastic tradition, twelve jovial friars
gave up their vocation for a questionable existence
on the flying trapeze.*

22/25 Point

Italian and French Italics

ABCDEFG
HIJKLMN
OPQRSTU
VWXYZ

abcdefghijklmnopqrstuvwxyz

äöüß § $ % & @ ?! . , . : ; *

1234567890

44 Point

Forsaking monastic tradition, twelve jovial friars gave up their
vocation for a questionable existence on the flying trapeze.

23/25 Point

ABCDEFG
HIJKLMN
OPQRSTU
VWXYZ

abcdefghijklmnopqrstuvwxyz

äöüßß§$@$?!.,.;*

1234567890

38 Point

Forsaking monastic tradition, twelve jovial friars
gave up their vocation for a questionable existence
on the flying trapeze.

20/25 Point

$$\mathscr{A} \; \mathscr{B} \; \mathscr{C} \; \mathscr{D} \; \mathscr{E} \; \mathscr{F} \; \mathscr{G}$$

$$\mathscr{H} \; \mathscr{I} \; \mathscr{J} \; \mathscr{K} \; \mathscr{L} \; \mathscr{M} \; \mathscr{N}$$

$$\mathscr{O} \; \mathscr{P} \; \mathscr{Q} \; \mathscr{R} \; \mathscr{S} \; \mathscr{T} \; \mathscr{U}$$

$$\mathscr{V} \; \mathscr{W} \; \mathscr{X} \; \mathscr{Y} \; \mathscr{Z}$$

abcdefghijklmnopqrstuvw

xyzäöüß& %$@ ?!.,.;*

1234567890

49 Point

Italian and French Italics

Forsaking monastic tradition, twelve jovial friars gave up their vocation for a questionable existence on the flying trapeze.

20/25 Point

ABCDEFG
HIJKLMN
OPQRSTU
VWXYZ
abcdefghijklmn
opqrstuvwxyzäöüß
&%$@?!.,.:;*
1234567890

50 Point

Forsaking monastic tradition, twelve jovial friars
gave up their vocation for a questionable existence
on the flying trapeze.

18/25 Point

Italian and French Italics

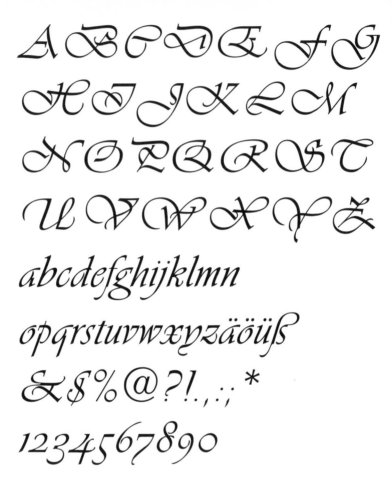

ABCDEFG
HIJKLM
NOPQRST
UVWXYZ
abcdefghijklmn
opqrstuvwxyzäöüß
&$%@?!.,.;*
1234567890

33 Point

Forsaking monastic tradition, twelve jovial
friars gave up their vocation for a questionable
existence on the flying trapeze.

18/25 Point

46 Point

Forsaking monastic tradition, twelve jovial friars gave up their vocation for a questionable existence on the flying trapeze.

24/25 Point

Italian and French Italics

A B C D E F G
H I J K L M N
O P Q R S T U
V W X Y Z

abcdefghijklmnopqrstuvwxyz

äöüß s$& @?!.,:;*

1234567890

44 Point

Forsaking monastic tradition, twelve jovial friars gave up their vocation for a questionable existence on the flying trapeze.

25/25 Point

Italian and French Italics

A B C D E F G H
I J K L M N O P Q
R S T U V W X Y Z

abcdefghijklmn

opqrstuvwxyz

äöüß@$&?!.,:;*

1234567890

48 Point

Forsaking monastic tradition, twelve jovial friars gave up their vocation for a questionable existence on the flying trapeze.

18/25 Point

CRESTED BUTTE

Wildflower Festival

JULY 6, 7, & 8 1990

Poster, Anonymous, 1990

A B C D E F G

H I J K L M N

N O P Q R S T

U V W X Y Z

abcdefghijklmn

opqrstuvwxyzäöüß

$ & ?!.,:;1234567890

44 Point

Forsaking monastic tradition, twelve jovial friars
gave up their vocation for a questionable existence
on the flying trapeze.

20/25 Point

Italian and French Italics

111

A B C D E F G
H I J K L M N
O P Q R S T U
V W X Y Z

abcdefghijklmnopqrstuvw
xyzäöüß&%$@?!.,.;
1234567890

48 Point

Forsaking monastic tradition, twelve jovial
friars gave up their vocation for a questionable
existence on the flying trapeze.

22/25 Point

Italian and French Italics

Book cover, Chip Kidd

Italian and French Italics

Kris Holmes, 1989 | linotype.com

ABCDEFGH

IJKLMNOPQ

RSTUVWXYZ

abcdefghijklmn

opqrstuvwxyz

äöüß&$%?!.,.:;*

1234567890

41 Point

Forsaking monastic tradition, twelve jovial friars gave up their vocation for a questionable existence on the flying trapeze.

16/25 Point

Manfred Klein, 2003 | moorstation.org | CD

A B C D E F G H I J
K L M N O P Q R
S T U V W X Y Z
a b c d e f g h i j k l m n
o p q r s t u v w x y z
á ö ü ß & $ § @ ? ! . , . ; *
1 2 3 4 5 6 7 8 9 0

45 Point

---

*Forsaking monastic tradition, twelve
jovial friars gave up their vocation for a
questionable existence on the flying trapeze.*

16/25 Point

Italian and French Italics

Linus Romer, 2009 | dafont.com | CD

47 Point

Forsaking monastic tradition, twelve jovial friars gave up their vocation for a questionable existence on the flying trapeze.

19/25 Point

ABCDEFG
HIJKLMN
OPQRSTU
VWXYZ
abcdefghijklmn
opqrstuvwxyz
äöüß&§@$?!.,,;;*
1234567890

38 Point

Forsaking monastic tradition, twelve
jovial friars gave up their vocation for a
questionable existence on the flying trapeze.

15/25 Point

Arno Drescher, 1936 | linotype.com

A B C D E F G
H I J K L M N
O P Q R S T U
V W X Y Z

abcdefghijklmn

opqrstuvwxyzäöüß

$%&@?!.,:; *

1234567890

42 Point

Forsaking monastic tradition, twelve jovial friars
gave up their vocation for a questionable existence
on the flying trapeze.

18/25 Point

Italian and French Italics

118

ABCDEFG
HIJKLMN
OPQRSJU
VWXYZ

abcdefghijklmn

opqrstuvwxyzäöüß

&@$?!.,.;*

1234567890

42 Point

Forsaking monastic tradition, twelve jovial friars gave up their vocation for a questionable existence on the flying trapeze.

18/25 Point

ABCDEFGHI
JKLMNOPQR
STUVWXYZ
abcdefghijklmn
opqrstuvwxyz
§&%$@?!.,:;*
1234567890

43 Point

Forsaking monastic tradition, twelve jovial friars gave up their vocation for a questionable existence on the flying trapeze.

14/25 Point

Italian and French Italics

ABCDEFGHIJ
KLMNOPQR
STUVWXYZ

abcdefghijklmn
opqrstuvwxyzäöüß
&$%@?!.,.;*
1234567890

52 Point

Forsaking monastic tradition, twelve jovial friars gave up their vocation for a questionable existence on the flying trapeze.

19/25 Point

Italian and French Italics

David Rakowski, 1992 | moorstation.org | CD

ABCDEFG
HIJKLMN
OPQRSTU
VWXYZ

abcdefghijklmn

opqrstuvwxyz

&?!.,:;1234567890

44 Point

Forsaking monastic tradition, twelve jovial friars gave up their vocation for a questionable existence on the flying trapeze.

18/25 Point

Italian and French Italics

Elisara **Autographis-Gert Wiescher, 2008 | myfonts.com**

A B C D E F G H

I J K L M N O P Q

R S T U V W X Y Z

abcdefghijklmnopqrstuvwxyz

äöüß § & $ % @ ? ! . , : ; *

1234567890

62 Point

Forsaking monastic tradition, twelve jovial friars gave up their vocation for a questionable existence on the flying trapeze.

30/25 Point

Le Fragole.

2.

Qualche tempo dopo passò per questo villag_
gio un Uffiziale di rango, che portava pa_
recchj distintivi d'onore. Si fermò colla su_
perba sua carrozza all'osteria per far da_
re da mangiar ai cavalli, ed avendo sentito
dire del soldato infermo, lo visitò.

Il vecchio Soldato gli raccontò subito
della sua benefattrice. "Che, esclamò l'Uffi_
ziale, una povera fanciulla ha fatto tanto per
te! Or io, che fui già tuo Generale, sotto a cui
hai servito, non posso neppur fare di meno.
Disporrò ben tosto, che tu alla meglio venga
alimentato all'osteria."

Lo fece, ed indi andò nella casa della
picciola Agata: Buona fanciulla, le dis_
se commosso, la tua beneficenza mi ha toc_
cato il cuore, e riempiuto gli occhi di lagrime.
Tu hai donato una dozzina di pezzi da sei
a quel vecchio guerriero; eccoti perciò altrettan_
te pezze d'oro." I Genitori stupefatti dissero:
"Quest'è troppo" ma il Generale soggiunse:
No, no! questa non è che una misera ricom_
pensa; una migliore s'el ha da aspettare la
buona ragazza su in cielo."

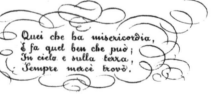

Quei che ha misericordia,
È fa quel ben che può;
In cielo e sulla terra,
Sempre mercè trovò.

Excerpt from the book *Le Fragole,* vol. 2,
by Christoph von Schmid, c. 1830

𝒜 ℬ 𝒞 𝒟 ℰ ℱ 𝒢
ℋ ℐ 𝒥 𝒦 ℒ ℳ 𝒩
𝒪 𝒫 𝒬 ℛ 𝒮 𝒯 𝒰
𝒱 𝒲 𝒳 𝒴 𝒵

abcdefghijklmm

opqrstuvwxyz

1234567890

55 Point

Forsaking monastic tradition, twelve jovial friars
gave up their vocation for a questionable existence
on the flying trapeze.

23/25 Point

Italian and French Italics

125

A B C D E F G
H I J K L M
N O P Q R S T
U V W X Y Z
abcdefghijklmn
opqrstuvwxyzäöüß
& $ § @ ? ! . , . ; *
1234567890

52 Point

Forsaking monastic tradition, twelve jovial friars gave up their vocation for a questionable existence on the flying trapeze.

20/24 Point

Italian and French Italics

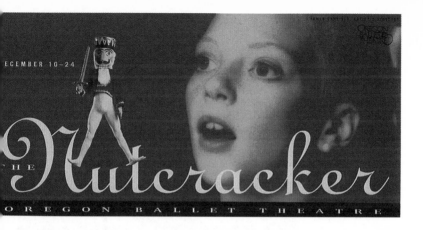

Advertising billboard,
Hal Wolverton, 1992

Brochure, Louise Fili, Jessica Hische, 2009

A B C D E F G
H I J K L M N
O P Q R S T U
V W X Y Z

abcdefghijklmnopqrstu
vwxyzäöü&$%@?!.,:;*
1234567890

38 Point

Forsaking monastic tradition, twelve jovial friars gave up their
vocation for a questionable existence on the flying trapeze.

15/25 Point

Italian and French Italics

129

Monotype Design Studio, 2005 | linotype.com

ABCDEFG
HIJKLMN
OPQRSTU
VWXYZ

abcdefghijklmnopqrstu
vwxyzäöüß&%$@?!.,:;*
1234567890

45 Point

Forsaking monastic tradition, twelve jovial friars
gave up their vocation for a questionable existence
on the flying trapeze.

22/24 Point

Louis Barbedor, 1646, Paris

Poster, *c.* 1933

Monotype Design Studio, 1931 | linotype.com

ABCDEFGHI

JKLMNOPQ

RSTUVWXYZ

abcdefghijklmn

opqrstuvwxyz

äöüß&$%₀?!.,:;*

1234567890

42 Point

---

*Forsaking monastic tradition, twelve
jovial friars gave up their vocation for a
questionable existence on the flying trapeze.*

17/25 Point

Italian and French Italics

133

ABCDEFG
HIJKLMN
OPQRSTU
VWXYZ
abcdefghijklmn
opqrstuvwxyzäöüß
&$%?!.,:;*
1234567890

44 Point

Forsaking monastic tradition, twelve jovial
friars gave up their vocation for a questionable
existence on the flying trapeze.

19/25 Point

ABCDEFGHI
JKLMNOPQR
STUVWXYZ
abcdefghijklmn
opqrstuvwxyzäöüß
§&%$@?!.,:;*
1234567890

44 Point

Forsaking monastic tradition, twelve jovial friars gave up their vocation for a questionable existence on the flying trapeze.

19/25 Point

Italian and French Italics

135

Dino dos Santos, 2007 | dstype.com

29 Point

Forsaking monastic tradition, twelve jovial friars gave up their vocation for a questionable existence on the flying trapeze.

14/25 Point

Handwriting
Regras Methodicas para se aprender a escrever os Caracteres das letras
Art de L'écriture
Ventura inventou
Penmanship
Escrita & Aritmética, Lisboa, 1820
Atlas Calligraphico

A virtude da caridade move as mais. Bemaventurados os misericordiosos. Christo padeceo, e morreo pelos homens. Ditozos aquelles, que vivem em Paz.

Ventura, Dino dos Santos, 2008

34 Point

Forsaking monastic tradition, twelve jovial friars gave up their vocation for a questionable existence on the flying trapeze.

15/25 Point

Insigne – Jeremy Dooley, 2006 | myfonts.com

ABCDEFG
HIJKLM
NOPQRST
VVWXYZ
abcdefghijklmn
opqrstuvwxyzäöü
$%@?!.,:;*
1234567890

44 Point

Forsaking monastic tradition, twelve jovial friars
gave up their vocation for a questionable existence on
the flying trapeze.

17/25 Point

Italian and French Italics

The Distinguished Elegance of a Pointed Nib

Thanks to the completely different nib and writing technique from which these script fonts are derived, they are easily identified. The pointed, flexible nib produces a varying thickness of line depending on the amount of pressure used, and is ideally suited for executing flourishes without snagging the paper.

This script can be easily engraved in copper plates, hence the term 'copperplate'. In the eighteenth century it became firmly established as the preferred script for official documents, largely due to the economic power of England.

This style of lettering soon became popular among the aristocracy – it was often used in invitations and steel-engraving for cards made from handmade paper stock. In America in the 1970s, its exuberant flourishes made a comeback as an iconic part of advertising, and today their use has a retro feel to it. It is easy to misjudge the type size with English script fonts: the ascenders and descenders often have twice the x-height of the lowercase letters! Other hallmarks of English script fonts include a marked slant to the right, oval forms and fluid transitions between thick and thin lines.

A B C D E F
G H I J K
L M N O P
Q R S T U
V W X Y Z
abcdefghijklmnopqrst
uvwxyz &$% @?!.,:;*
1234567890

41 Point

Forsaking monastic tradition, twelve jovial
friars gave up their vocation for a questionable
existence on the flying trapeze.

19/25 Point

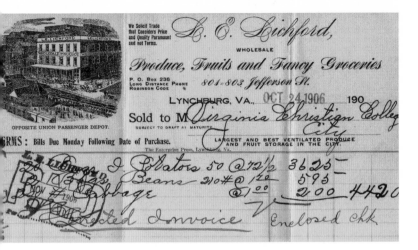

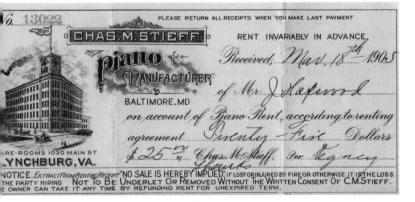

Above: Receipt, 1906. Below: Receipt, 1905

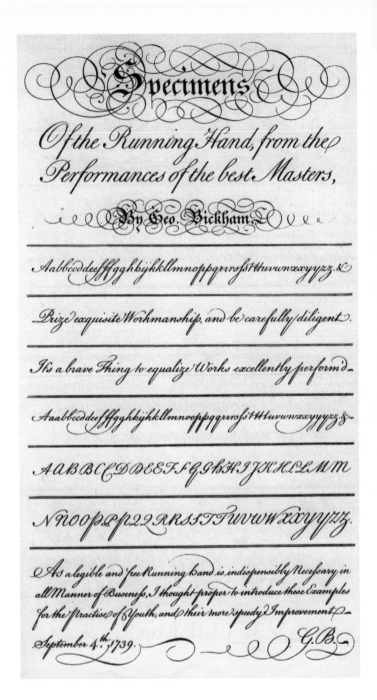

From *The Universal Penman*,
by George Bickham, 1740s

A B C D E F G
H I J K L M N
O P Q R S T
U V W X Y Z
abcdefghijklmn
opqrstuvwxyzäöüß
§ $ & @ ?! .,:; *
1234567890

55 Point

Forsaking monastic tradition, twelve jovial
friars gave up their vocation for a questionable
existence on the flying trapeze.

24/25 Point

English Copperplate

149

Hans Bohn, 1957 | linotype.com

A B C D E F G

H I J K L M N

O P Q R S T U

V W X Y Z

abcdefghijklmn

opqrstuvwxyzäöüß

&§$%?!.,.:;   *

1234567890

40 Point

English Copperplate

*Forsaking monastic tradition, twelve jovial friars
gave up their vocation for a questionable existence
on the flying trapeze.*

22/25 Point

A B C D E F G
H I J K L M
N O P Q R S T
U V W X Y Z
abcdefghijklmn
opqrstuvwxyzäöüß
§$%&?!@.,.;*
1234567890

37 Point

Forsaking monastic tradition, twelve jovial friars
gave up their vocation for a questionable existence
on the flying trapeze.

17/25 Point

English Copperplate

151

$\mathcal{A} \ \mathcal{B} \ \mathcal{C} \ \mathcal{D} \ \mathcal{E} \ \mathcal{F} \ \mathcal{G}$

$\mathcal{H} \ \mathcal{I} \ \mathcal{J} \ \mathcal{K} \ \mathcal{L} \ \mathcal{M} \ \mathcal{N}$

$\mathcal{O} \ \mathcal{P} \ \mathcal{Q} \ \mathcal{R} \ \mathcal{S} \ \mathcal{T} \ \mathcal{U}$

$\mathcal{V} \ \mathcal{W} \ \mathcal{X} \ \mathcal{Y} \ \mathcal{Z}$

abcdefghijklmn

opqrstuvwxyzäöüß

&$%@?!.,.:; *

1234567890

42 Point

Forsaking monastic tradition, twelve jovial friars gave up their vocation for a questionable existence on the flying trapeze.

18/25 Point

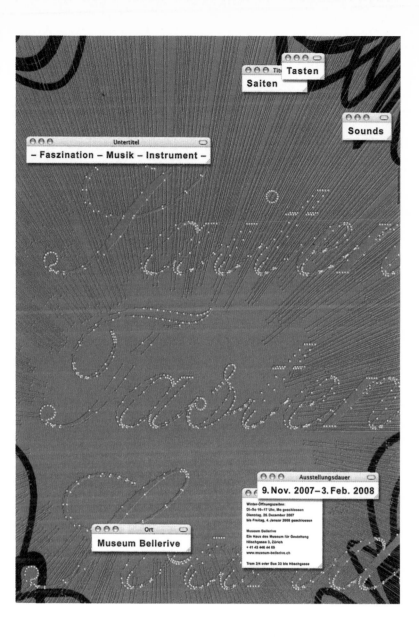

Poster, Sandro Wettstein, 2007

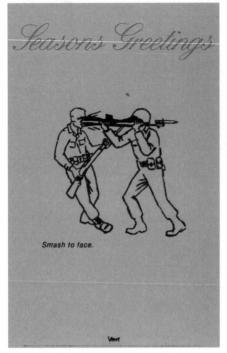

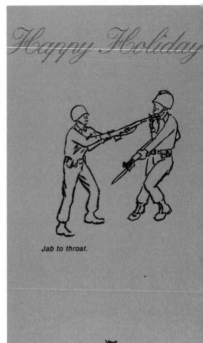

Cards, Todd Fedell and Russ Haan, 1995

A B C D E F G

H I J K L M N

O P Q R S T U

V W X Y Z

abcdefghijklmn

opqrstuvwxyzäöüß

$ % § & ? ! . , . ; ＊

1234567890

40 Point

Forsaking monastic tradition, twelve jovial friars

gave up their vocation for a questionable existence

on the flying trapeze.

15/25 Point

English Copperplate

155

American Greetings Corporation, 1996
abstractfonts.com | CD

ABCDEFGH
IJKLMNOPQ
RSTUVWXYZ
abcdefghijklmn
opqrstuvwxyzäöüß
*$%&@?!.,.:; ***
1234567890

47 Point

Forsaking monastic tradition, twelve jovial friars
gave up their vocation for a questionable existence
on the flying trapeze.

20/25 Point

English Copperplate

156

profonts, 2009 | urwpp.de

ABCDEFG
HIJKLM
NOPQRST
UVWXYZ
abcdefghijklmn
opqrstuvwxyz
äöüß§&$%?!.,:;
1234567890

39 Point

Forsaking monastic tradition, twelve jovial friars
gave up their vocation for a questionable existence on
the flying trapeze.

15/25 Point

English Copperplate

Morris Fuller Benton, 1888 | myfonts.com

A B C D E F G H I

J K L M N O P Q R

S T U V W X Y Z

abcdefghijklmn

opqrstuvwxyzäöüß

&$%@?!.,:; *

1234567890

43 Point

Forsaking monastic tradition, twelve jovial
friars gave up their vocation for a questionable
existence on the flying trapeze.

16/25 Point

Poster, Sabine Schmid, Lutz Widmaier, 2005

Matthew Carter, 1972 | linotype.com

A B C D E F G
H I J K L M N
O P Q R S T U
V W X Y Z
abcdefghijklmn
opqrstuvwxyzäöüß
§&$% @?!.,.; *
1234567890

43 Point

Forsaking monastic tradition, twelve jovial friars
gave up their vocation for a questionable existence
on the flying trapeze.

18/25 Point

160

A B C D E F G
H I J K L M N
O P Q R S T U
V W X Y Z
abcdefghijklmn
opqrstuvwxyz
äöüß&$%@?!.,.:; *
1234567890

43 Point

Forsaking monastic tradition, twelve
jovial friars gave up their vocation for a
questionable existence on the flying trapeze.

17/25 Point

English Copperplate

161

41 Point

Forsaking monastic tradition, twelve jovial friars
gave up their vocation for a questionable
existence on the flying trapeze.

17/25 Point

Hermann Zapf, Akira Kobayashi, 2009 | linotype.com

A B C D E F G
H I J K L M N
O P Q R S T U
V W X Y Z
abcdefghijklmn
opqrstuvwxyzäöüß
&$%@?!.,.:; *
1234567890

40 Point

Forsaking monastic tradition, twelve jovial friars gave
up their vocation for a questionable existence on the
flying trapeze.

16/25 Point

English Copperplate

texte et mise en scène Marielle Pinsard
26 janvier au 4 février 2007

Poster, Giorgio Pesce, 2007

Edward Benguiat, 1994 | linotype.com

40 Point

Forsaking monastic tradition, twelve jovial friars gave up their vocation for a questionable existence on the flying trapeze.

20/25 Point

A B C D E F G
H I J K L M N
O P Q R S T U
V W X Y Z
abcdefghijklmn
opqrstuvwxyzäöüß
§&%@$?!.,.;*
1234567890

40 Point

English Copperplate

Forsaking monastic tradition, twelve jovial friars
gave up their vocation for a questionable existence
on the flying trapeze.

15/25 Point

Poster, Werner Celand, 2008

Poster, Don Miller, 1996

American Greetings Corporation, 1996

abstractfonts.com | CD

ABCDEFGH

IJKLMNOPQ

RSTUVWXYZ

abcdefghijklmn

opqrstuvwxyzäöüß

&$%@?!.,.;; *

1234567890

44 Point

Forsaking monastic tradition, twelve jovial friars
gave up their vocation for a questionable existence
on the flying trapeze.

20/25 Point

English Copperplate

Monotype Design Studio, 2003 | linotype.com

A B C D E F G
H I J K L M N
O P Q R S T U
V W X Y Z

abcdefghijklmn

opqrstuvwxyzäöüß

§§%& @?!.,;: *

1234567890

41 Point

English Copperplate

Forsaking monastic tradition, twelve jovial
friars gave up their vocation for a questionable
existence on the flying trapeze.

20/25 Point

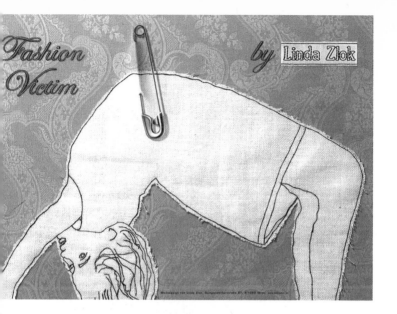

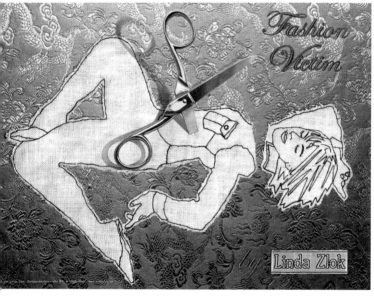

Posters, Thomas Schmid, Isabella Diessel,
Norbert Hovath, 2003

Degree show poster, Gerda Raidt, 2002

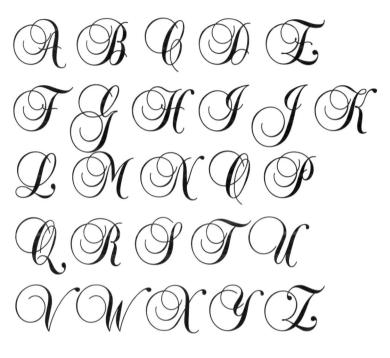

A B C D E
F G H I J K
L M N O P
Q R S T U
V W X Y Z

abcdefghijklmnopqrstuvwxyzäöüß

&$%?!.,:;*1234567890

52 Point

---

*Forsaking monastic tradition, twelve jovial friars
gave up their vocation for a questionable existence
on the flying trapeze.*

30/25 Point

English Copperplate

Donald Stevens, 1978 | linotype.com

A B C D E F G
H I J K L M N
O P Q R S T U
V W X Y Z
abcdefghijklmnopqrstuvwxyz
*äöüß & $ % ? ! . , . ; *
1 2 3 4 5 6 7 8 9 0

42 Point

Forsaking monastic tradition, twelve jovial friars gave up their vocation for a questionable existence on the flying trapeze.

25/25 Point

English Copperplate

174

David Quay, 1987 | linotype.com

A B C D E F G H
I J K L M N O P Q
R S T U V W X Y Z
abcdefghijklmn
opqrstuvwxyzäöüß
§&?!.,:; * 1234567890

60 Point

Forsaking monastic tradition, twelve jovial friars
gave up their vocation for a questionable existence
on the flying trapeze.

28/25 Point

English Copperplate

175

Monotype Design Studio, 1938 | linotype.com

ABCDEFGHI

JKLMNOPQ

RSTUVWXYZ

abcdefghijklmn

opqrstuvwxyzäöüß

&$%@?!.,.;*

1234567890

56 Point

Forsaking monastic tradition, twelve jovial
friars gave up their vocation for a questionable
existence on the flying trapeze.

24/25 Point

English Copperplate

176

Milk

The Surprising Story of Milk Through the Ages

with 120 adventurous Recipes that Explore the riches of our First Food

Anne Mendelson

Book cover, Barbara deWilde, 2009

ABCDEFGHIJ
KLMNOPQR
STUVWXYZ
abcdefghijklmn
opqrstuvwxyzäöüß
&$%?!.,;:*
1234567890

43 Point

Forsaking monastic tradition, twelve jovial friars
gave up their vocation for a questionable existence
on the flying trapeze.

17/25 Point

A B C D E F G H I J
K L M N O P Q R
S T U V W X Y Z

a b c d e f g h i j k l m n o p q r s t u v

w x y z ä ö ü ß & $ % @ ? ! . , : ; *

1 2 3 4 5 6 7 8 9 0

51 Point

Forsaking monastic tradition, twelve jovial
friars gave up their vocation for a questionable
existence on the flying trapeze.

30/25 Point

Richard Lipton, 1994 | myfonts.com

A B C D E F
G H I J K
L M N O P Q
R S T U
V W X Y Z

abcdefghijklmn

opqrstuvwxyzäöüß

*§$&% @?!.,.,:; * 1234567890*

40 Point

*Forsaking monastic tradition, twelve jovial friars
gave up their vocation for a questionable existence
on the flying trapeze.*

22/25 Point

A B C D E
F G H I J
K L M N O
P Q R S T
U V W X Y Z

a b c d e f g h i j k l m n

o p q r s t u v w x y z ä ö ü ß

*& $ % . ? ! , . : ; * 1 2 3 4 5 6 7 8 9 0*

40 Point

---

*Forsaking monastic tradition, twelve jovial
friars gave up their vocation for a questionable
existence on the flying trapeze.*

20/25 Point

Hideki Katayama | abstractfonts.com | CD

40 Point

Forsaking monastic tradition, twelve
jovial friars gave up their vocation for a
questionable existence on the flying trapeze.

14/20 Point

English Copperplate

Poster, Henryk Tomaszewski, 1947

Monotype Design Studio, 1999 | linotype.com

44 Point

Forsaking monastic tradition, twelve jovial friars gave up their vocation for a questionable existence on the flying trapeze.

24/24 Point

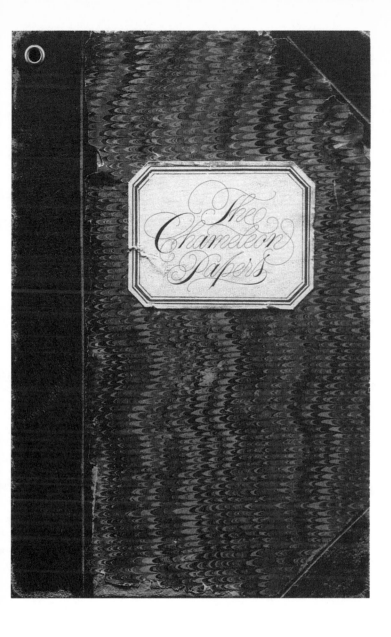

The Chameleon Papers, Bruce
McIntosh, Robert Cipriani, 1982

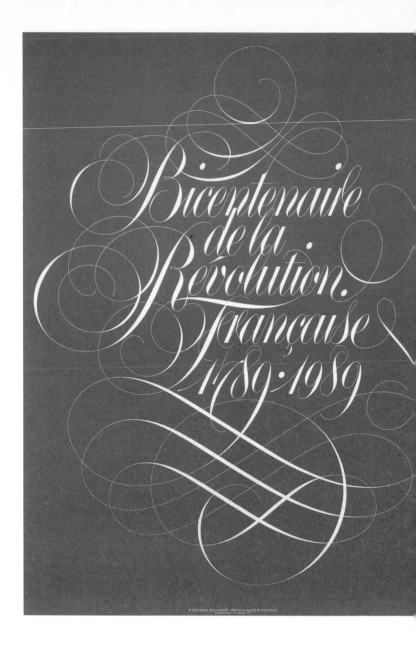

Poster, Jean Larcher, Cergy, 1989

Panos Vassiliou, 2007 | parachute.gr

A B C D E F G
H I J K L M N
O P Q R S T U
V W X Y Z

abcdefghijklmnopqrstuvwxyz

äöüß& $% @ ?!.,.;*

1234567890

33 Point

Forsaking monastic tradition, twelve jovial friars gave up their vocation for a questionable existence on the flying trapeze.

22/25 Point

49 Point

Forsaking monastic tradition, twelve jovial friars
gave up their vocation for a questionable existence
on the flying trapeze.

24/25 Point

English Copperplate

188

Magazine spread, Nancy Harris Rouemy, 2008

Hermann Ihlenburg, Rebecca Alaccari, 2007
canadatype.com

A B C D E F G H I

J K L M N O P Q

R S T U V W X Y Z

a b c d e f g h i j k l m n

o p q r s t u v w x y z

*ä ö ü ß & $ % a) ? ! . , . ; *

1 2 3 4 5 6 7 8 9 0

40 Point

Forsaking monastic tradition, twelve jovial
friars gave up their vocation for a questionable
existence on the flying trapeze.

16/25 Point

English Copperplate

190

Helmut Matheis, Rebecca Alaccari, 2006 | canadatype.com

ABCDEFG
HIJKLMN
OPQRSTU
VWXYZ

abcdefghijklmn

opqrstuvwxyzäöüß

&%@$?!.,.;

1234567890

35 Point

Forsaking monastic tradition, twelve jovial friars
gave up their vocation for a questionable existence
on the flying trapeze.

17/25 Point

English Copperplate

The Penthouse Calendar, 1980

The Mighty Pete, 2008 | myfonts.com

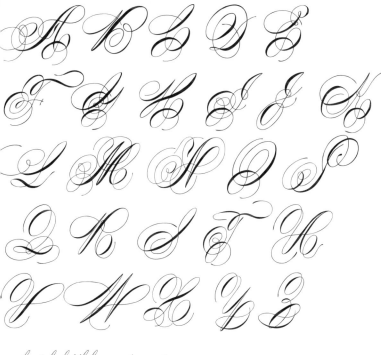

abcdefghijklmnopqrstuvwxyz

äöü ß & $ %₀ ? ! . ,.;: * 1234567890

40 Point

Forsaking monastic tradition, twelve jovial friars gave up their vocation for a questionable existence on the flying trapeze.

36/25 Point

45 Point

Forsaking monastic tradition, twelve jovial friars gave up their vocation for a questionable existence on the flying trapeze.

30/24 Point

Burgues script, Alejandro Paul, 2008

Poster, Stefan Sagmeister
and Matthias Ernstberger, 2005

Doyald Young, 1984 | linotype.com

46 Point

Forsaking monastic tradition, twelve jovial friars gave up their vocation for a questionable existence on the flying trapeze.

25/25 Point

A B C D E F

G H I J K

L M N O P

Q R S T U

V W X Y Z

abcdefghijklmnopqrstuvwxyz

*äöüß&@ §$?!.,:, * 1234567890*

33 Point

English Copperplate

*Forsaking monastic tradition, twelve jovial friars
gave up their vocation for a questionable existence
on the flying trapeze.*

18/24 Point

198

Poster, Elisabeth Plass,
Katrin Adamaszek, 2008

With a Brush and a Flourish

The practice of writing with brushes has its origins in Asia. Europeans later discovered this technique for themselves, using it to put a new spin on their scripts. When executed with a brush, a script takes on an entirely different quality that is easily identifiable. The tremors of the writer's hand are transferred to the brush, and when combined with uneven pressure this creates a very mobile line. Brush scripts were mostly used in lead typesetting to imitate advertising placards and to lend a fresh, current sensibility: fonts like 'Reporter No. 2' (see page 271) are familiar from film posters and newspaper ads.

Ornate swash characters were used in lead typesetting from the end of the nineteenth century, in an attempt to compete with lithography. Many scripts also included decorative alternatives to the plain capital letters, which took on increasingly elaborate forms, virtually to the point of illegibility – this tradition continues to this day in many digital fonts.

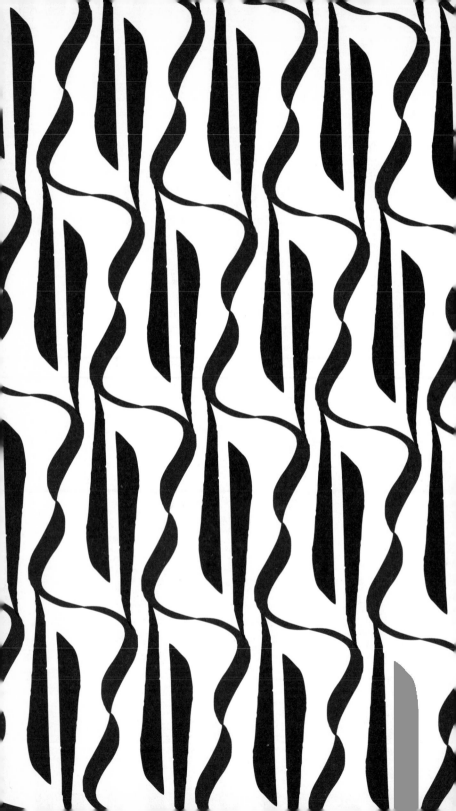

GBCDE7GHIJ
KLMNOPQR
STUVWXY3
abcdefghijklmn
opqrstuvwxyzäöüß
§$&%@?!.,:;*
1234567890

45 Point

Forsaking monastic tradition, twelve jovial friars gave up their vocation for a questionable existence on the flying trapeze.

18/25 Point

ABCDEFGH
IJKLMNOPQ
RSTUVWXYZ
abcdefghijklmn
opqrstuvwxyz
$%&@?!.,:;*
1234567890

56 Point

Forsaking monastic tradition, twelve jovial friars
gave up their vocation for a questionable existence
on the flying trapeze.

23/25 Point

Brush & Swash

ABCDEFGHIJ
KLMNOPQR
STUVWXYZ
abcdefghijk
lmnopqrstuv
wxyzäöüß
&§@%$?!.,.;*
1234567890

46 Point

---

*Forsaking monastic tradition, twelve jovial
friars gave up their vocation for a questionable
existence on the flying trapeze.*

15/25 Point

Gary D. Jessey, 1992 | urbanfonts.com | CD

ABCDEFGH
IJKLMNOPQ
RSTUVWXYZ
abcdefghijklmn
opqrstuvwxyz
$&?!.,:; *
1234567890

45 Point

Forsaking monastic tradition, twelve
jovial friars gave up their vocation for a
questionable existence on the flying trapeze.

16/25 Point

Brush & Swash

Poster, William Thompson, 1997

Patty King, 1995 | linotype.com

ABCDEFGHIJ

KLMNOPQR

STUVWXYZ

abcdefghijklmn

opqrstuvwxyzäöüß

&%$@?!.,:;*

1234567890

43 Point

Forsaking monastic tradition, twelve jovial friars
gave up their vocation for a questionable existence
on the flying trapeze.

17/25 Point

Brush & Swash

A B C D E F G H I J
K L M N O P Q R
S T U V W X Y Z
abcdefghijklmn
opqrstuvwxyz
äöüß&$%@?!.,:;*
1234567890

48 Point

Forsaking monastic tradition, twelve jovial friars
gave up their vocation for a questionable existence
on the flying trapeze.

15/24 Point

ABCDEFGH
IJKLMNOPQ
RSTUVWXYZ
abcdefghijk
lmnopqrstu
vwxyzäöüß
$%§&@?!.,:;*
1234567890

43 Point

Forsaking monastic tradition, twelve jovial friars
gave up their vocation for a questionable existence
on the flying trapeze.

14/25 Point

Brush & Swash

ABCDEFG
HIJKLMN
OPQRSTU
VWXYZ
abcdefghijklmn
opqrstuvwxyz
äöüß$&?!.,:; *
1234567890

43 Point

Forsaking monastic tradition, twelve jovial
friars gave up their vocation for a questionable
existence on the flying trapeze.

15/25 Point

Brush & Swash

Arts & Letters Corporation | Bossfonts.com | CD

A B C D E F G
H I J K L M N
O P Q R S T U
V W X Y Z

abcdefghijklmn

opqrstuvwxyz

§$%&?!.,:;*

1234567890

40 Point

Forsaking monastic tradition, twelve jovial friars

gave up their vocation for a questionable existence

on the flying trapeze.

14/25 Point

Brush & Swash

ABCDEFGH
JJKLMNOPQ
RSTUVWXYZ
abcdefghijklmn
opqrstuvwxyzäöüß
&%)(?!.,:;*
1234567890

47 Point

Forsaking monastic tradition, twelve jovial friars gave up their
vocation for a questionable existence on the flying trapeze.

18/25 Point

Brush & Swash

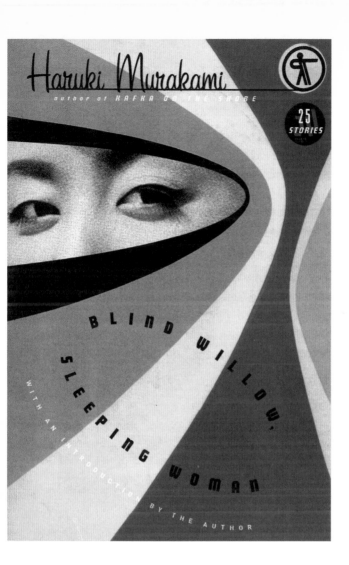

Haruki Murakami

author of KAFKA ON THE SHORE

25 STORIES

BLIND WILLOW, SLEEPING WOMAN

WITH AN INTRODUCTION BY THE AUTHOR

Book cover, Alfred A. Knopf, 2006

Poster, anonymous, 1996

Robert E. Smith, 1942 | linotype.com

A B C D E F G
H I J K L M N
O P Q R S T U
V W X Y Z
abcdefghijklmn
opqrstuvwxyzäöüß
&§%?!.,:;*
1234567890

41 Point

Forsaking monastic tradition, twelve jovial friars
gave up their vocation for a questionable existence
on the flying trapeze.

15/25 Point

Dieter Steffmann | moorstation.org | CD

ABCDEFGH
IJKLMNOPQ
RSTUVWXYZ

abcdefghijklmnopqrstuvwxyz

äöüß&$@?!.,:;*

1234567890

51 Point

Forsaking monastic tradition, twelve jovial friars gave up
their vocation for a questionable existence on the flying trapeze.

22/25 Point

Poster, Stephan Bundi, 2008

221

American Greetings Corporation, 1996
abstractfonts.com | CD

A B C D E F G
H I J K L M N
O P Q R S T U
V W X Y Z

abcdefghijklmn
opqrstuvwxyzäöüß
&$%?!.,;: *
1234567890

43 Point

Forsaking monastic tradition, twelve
jovial friars gave up their vocation for a
questionable existence on the flying trapeze.

22/25 Point

A B C D E F G
H I J K L M N
O P Q R S T U
V W X Y Z
a b c d e f g h i j k l m n
o p q r s t u v w x y z ä ö ü ß
ß & $ % ? ! . , ; ; *
1 2 3 4 5 6 7 8 9 0

41 Point

Forsaking monastic tradition, twelve jovial friars
gave up their vocation for a questionable existence on
the flying trapeze.

20/25 Point

Brush & Swash

Book cover, Piet Schreuders, August 1984

Phill Grimshaw (1997), Roger Excoffon (1955) | linotype.com

ABCDEFGHIJ
KLMNOPQR
STUVWXYZ
abcdefghijklmn
opqrstuvwxyz
äöüß&$%?!.,:;*
1234567890

47 Point

Forsaking monastic tradition, twelve jovial
friars gave up their vocation for a questionable
existence on the flying trapeze.

17/25 Point

ABCDEFGHI
JKLMNOPQR
STUVWXYZ
abcdefghijk
lmnopqrstu
vwxyzäöüß
&%§$@?!.,:; *
1234567890

39 Point

Forsaking monastic tradition, twelve jovial
friars gave up their vocation for a questionable
existence on the flying trapeze.

13/25 Point

ABCDEFGHIJ
KLMNOPQR
STUVWXYZ

abcdefghijklmn
opqrstuvwxyz
äöüß$%&@?!.,:;*
1234567890

46 Point

Forsaking monastic tradition, twelve
jovial friars gave up their vocation for a
questionable existence on the flying trapeze.

16/25 Point

Brush & Swash

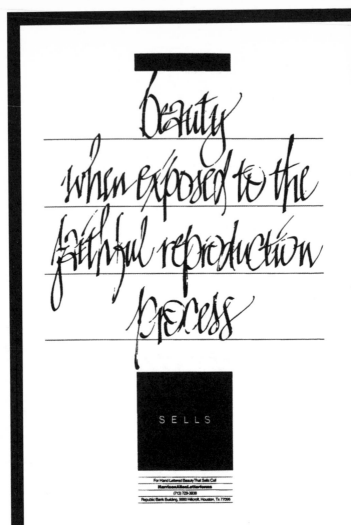

Promotional poster, Harrison Allen, 1989

Daniel Zadorozny, 2001 | iconian.com | CD

A B C D E F G H I J
K L M N O P Q R S T
U V W X Y Z

A B C D E F G H I J
K L M N O P Q R S T
U V W X Y Z

$ /) (S ! . , . ; :
1 2 3 4 5 6 7 8 9 0

34 Point

FORSAKING MONASTIC TRADITION, TWELVE JOVIAL
FRIARS GAVE UP THEIR VOCATION FOR A QUESTIONABLE
EXISTENCE ON THE FLYING TRAPEZE.

10/25 Point

Brush & Swash

ABCDEFGH

IJKLMNOPQ

RSTUVWXYZ

abcdefghijklmn

opqrstuvwxyz

äöüß&$@?!.,:;*

1234567890

41 Point

Forsaking monastic tradition, twelve jovial friars
gave up their vocation for a questionable existence
on the flying trapeze.

14/25 Point

Angel Koziupa, Alejandro Paul, 2007 | myfonts.com

ABCDEFGHIJ
KLMNOPQR
STUVWXYZ
abcdefghijklmn
opqrstuvwxyz
äöüß$&@?!.,:;*
1234567890

42 Point

Forsaking monastic tradition, twelve jovial friars
gave up their vocation for a questionable existence
on the flying trapeze.

16/25 Point

Brush & Swash

231

Nick Curtis, 1999 | nicksfonts.com | CD

ABCDEFG
HIJKLMN
OPQRSTU
VWXYZ
abcdefghijklmn
opqrstuvwxyz
äöüßE@?!.,:;*
1234567890

41 Point

---

*Forsaking monastic tradition, twelve
jovial friars gave up their vocation for a
questionable existence on the flying trapeze.*

14/20 Point

Poster, Niklaus Stoecklin, 1927

Page of a book,
Gail Anderson, Ken Delago, 2001

R. Casady, R. Ware, M. Wright | fontspace.com | CD

A B C D E F G
H I J K L M N
O P Q R S T U
V W X Y Z

abcdefghijklmn
opqrstuvwxyz
äöüß&%$?!,.;*
1234567890

49 Point

Forsaking monastic tradition, twelve jovial
friars gave up their vocation for a questionable
existence on the flying trapeze.

19/25 Point

Brush & Swash

235

ABCDEFG
HIJKLMN
OPQRSTU
VWXYZ
abcdefghijklmn
opqrstuvwxyz
äöüß§&$@?!.,.:;*
1234567890

42 Point

Forsaking monastic tradition, twelve jovial friars
gave up their vocation for a questionable existence
on the flying trapeze.

17/25 Point

Brush & Swash

Sam Wang, 1993 | fontspace.com | CD

ABCDEFGH
IJKLMNOPQ
RSTUVWXYZ
abcdefghijklmn
opqrstuvwxyz
&%@?!.,:;*
1234567890

44 Point

Forsaking monastic tradition, twelve jovial friars
gave up their vocation for a questionable existence
on the flying trapeze.

17/25 Point

Brush & Swash

237

Advertising poster, 1938

ABCDEFG
HIJKLMN
OPQRST
UVWXYZ
abcdefghijklmn
opqrstuvwxyz
&?!.,:;
1234567890

41 Point

Forsaking monastic tradition, twelve
jovial friars gave up their vocation for a
questionable existence on the flying trapeze.

15/25 Point

Brush & Swash

ABCDEFG
HIJKLMN
OPQRST
UVWXYZ

abcdefghijklmn
opqrstuvwxyzäöüß
$&%@?!.,:;*
1234567890

40 Point

Forsaking monastic tradition, twelve jovial friars
gave up their vocation for a questionable existence
on the flying trapeze.

19/25 Point

Book cover, Roberto de Vicq de Cumptich, 2009

241

ABCDEFGH
IJKLMNOPQ
RSTUVWXYZ
abcdefghijklmn
opqrstuvwxyzäöü
&$?!.,.;*
1234567890

43 Point

Forsaking monastic tradition, twelve jovial friars
gave up their vocation for a questionable existence
on the flying trapeze.

15/25 Point

Brush & Swash

A B C D E F G
H I J K L M N
O P Q R S T U
V W X Y Z

abcdefghijklmn

opqrstuvwxyzäöüß

&%$@?!.,:,*

1234567890

40 Point

Forsaking monastic tradition, twelve
jovial friars gave up their vocation for a
questionable existence on the flying trapeze.

18/25 Point

Brush & Swash

243

ABCDEFGHIJ
KLMNOPQR
STUVWXYZ
abcdefghijklmno
pqrstuvwxyzäöüß
§&$@?!.,:;*
1234567890

43 Point

Forsaking monastic tradition, twelve
jovial friars gave up their vocation for a
questionable existence on the flying trapeze.

15/24 Point

Brush & Swash

GET NEW *glasses* IN LESS THAN *five* MINUTES.

Buy a Coke float for just $1.49 and the classic Coke® glass it comes in is **FREE**. *always* **FRESHER!**

Advertising poster, Steven Sandstrom, 1996

Magazine cover, Nancy Harris Rouemy, 2009

ABCDEFG
HIJKLMN
OPQRSTU
VWXYZ
abcdefghijklmn
opqrstuvwxyz
äöüß$@&?!.,:;*
1234567890

33 Point

Forsaking monastic tradition, twelve
jovial friars gave up their vocation for a
questionable existence on the flying trapeze.

11/24 Point

ABCDEFG
HIJKLMNN
OPQRSTU
VWXYZ
abcdefghijk
lmnopqrstu
vwxyz&$?!.,:;*
1234567890

37 Point

Forsaking monastic tradition, twelve

jovial friars gave up their vocation for a

questionable existence on the flying trapeze.

12/25 Point

Linotype, 2010 | linotype.com

ABCDEFG
HIJKLMN
OPQRSTU
VWXYZ
abcdefghijklmn
opqrstuvwxyz
äöüß$@&?!.,:;*
1234567890

48 Point

Forsaking monastic tradition, twelve jovial friars
gave up their vocation for a questionable existence
on the flying trapeze.

17/25 Point

Brush & Swash

Phill Grimshaw, 1995 | linotype.com

ABCDEFGHI
JKLMNOPQ
RSTUVWXYZ
abcdefghijklmn
opqrstuvwxyzäöüß
&$%?!.,:;*
1234567890

40 Point

Forsaking monastic tradition, twelve jovial friars
gave up their vocation for a questionable existence
on the flying trapeze.

15/25 Point

Brush & Swash

250

Hans J. Zinken | myfont.de | CD

ABCDEFGH
IJKLMNOPQ
RSTUVWXYZ
abcdefghijklmn
opqrstuvwxyzåöñß
$%&?!.,:;*
1234567890

35 Point

Forsaking monastic tradition, twelve jovial friars
gave up their vocation for a questionable existence
on the flying trapeze.

13/25 Point

Brush & Swash

ABCDEFGHIJ
KLMNOPQR
STUVWXYZ
abcdefghijklmn
opqrstuvwxyz
%$@&?!.,:;*
1234567890

47 Point

Forsaking monastic tradition, twelve
jovial friars gave up their vocation for a
questionable existence on the flying trapeze.

17/25 Point

Chocolate
Truffles

COCOLAT

Fine Chocolates and Extraordinary Desserts

Endangered
Giant Panda

COCOLAT

Fine Chocolates and Extraordinary Desserts

Milk Chocolate
Eggplant

COCOLAT

Fine Chocolates and Extraordinary Desserts

Chocolate
Decadence

COCOLAT

Fine Chocolates and Extraordinary Desserts

Posters, Paul Curtin, Benta Lloyd, 1993

Jeroen van Ham, 2009 | joebob.nl

ABCDEFGHIJ

JKLMNOPQR

STUVWXYZ

abcdefghijklmn

opqrstuvwxyzääöüß

%$@&?!.,:;*

1234567890

38 Point

Forsaking monastic tradition, twelve
jovial friars gave up their vocation for a
questionable existence on the flying trapeze.

16/25 Point

Brush & Swash

ABCDEFGHI
JKLMNOPQR
STUVWXYZ
abcdefghijklmn
opqrstuvwxyzäöüß
%$@&?!.,.;*
1234567890

43 Point

Forsaking monastic tradition, twelve jovial friars
gave up their vocation for a questionable existence
on the flying trapeze.

15/25 Point

Brush & Swash

ABCDEFGH
IJKLMNOPQ
RSTUVWXYZ
abcdefghijklmn
opqrstuvwxyzäöüß
&$§%@?!.,:;*
1234567890

42 Point

Forsaking monastic tradition, twelve jovial
friars gave up their vocation for a questionable
existence on the flying trapeze.

16/25 Point

Guido Bittner, 2003 | linotype.com

ABCDEFGHIJ
KLMNOPQRS
TUVWXYZ
abcdefghijklmn
opqrstuvwxyzäöüß
$£%&@?!.,:;*
1234567890

40 Point

Forsaking monastic tradition, twelve
jovial friars gave up their vocation for a
questionable existence on the flying trapeze.

17/25 Point

Brush & Swash

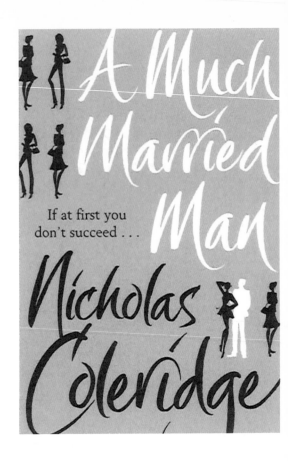

A Much Married Man

If at first you don't succeed . . .

Nicholas Coleridge

Book cover, Orion Publishing Group, 2006

A B C D E F G
H I J K L M N
O P Q R S T U
V W X Y Z

a b c d e f g h i j k l m n o p q r
s t u v w x y z ä ö ü ß fi fl
§ % & @ ? ! . , ; : *
1 2 3 4 5 6 7 8 9 0

47 Point

Forsaking monastic tradition, twelve jovial friars
gave up their vocation for a questionable existence
on the flying trapeze.

24/25 Point

Brush & Swash

ABCDEFG
HIJKLMN
OPQRSTU
VWXYZ

abcdefghijklmnopqrstuvwxyz

äöüß&$%@?!.,:;*

1234567890

36 Point

Forsaking monastic tradition, twelve jovial friars gave up their vocation for a questionable existence on the flying trapeze.

16/25 Point

46 Point

Forsaking monastic tradition, twelve jovial friars
gave up their vocation for a questionable existence
on the flying trapeze.

18/25 Point

ABCDEFG
HIJKLM
NOPQRST
UVWXYZ

abcdefghijklmn

opqrstuvwxyzäöüß

$%&@?!.,.;*

1234567890

41 Point

Forsaking monastic tradition, twelve jovial friars
gave up their vocation for a questionable existence
on the flying trapeze.

18/25 Point

A B C D E F G
H I J K L M
N O P Q R S
T U V W X Y Z

abcdefghijklmn
opqrstuvwxyzäöüß
$%&@?!.,:;*
1234567890

40 Point

ƒorsaking monastic tradition, twelve jovial
friars gave up their vocation for a questionable
existence on the flying trapeze.

18/25 Point

ABCDEFG
HIJKLMN
OPQRSTU
VWXYZ
abcdefghijklmn
opqrstuvwxyzäöüß
§&$@?!.,:;*
1234567890

35 Point

ℐorsaking monastic tradition, twelve jovial
friars gave up their vocation for a questionable
existence on the flying trapeze.

14/25 Point

ABCDEFG
HIJKLMN
OPQRSTU
VWXYZ
abcdefghijklmn
opqrstuvwxyz
äöüß&@$!!.,:;*
1234567890

43 Point

Forsaking monastic tradition, twelve jovial friars
gave up their vocation for a questionable existence
on the flying trapeze.

15/25 Point

Brush & Swash

265

ABCDEFGHIJ
KLMNOPQR
STUVWXYZ
abcdefghijklmn
opqrstuvwxyzäöüß
§$&%@?!.,.;*
1234567890

49 Point

Forsaking monastic tradition, twelve jovial friars gave

up their vocation for a questionable existence on the

flying trapeze.

16/25 Point

Poster, anonymous, 2003

Roger Excoffon, 1953 | linotype.com

ABCDEFGHIJ
KLMNOPQRS
TUVWXYZ
abcdefghijklmn
opqrstuvwxyzäöüß
§&$@?!.,:;*
1234567890

47 Point

Forsaking monastic tradition, twelve jovial friars
gave up their vocation for a questionable existence
on the flying trapeze.

17/25 Point

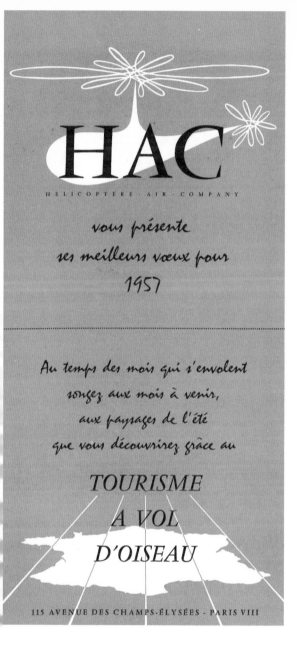

Specimen sheet, advertisement, 1957

Väter, die Zukunft eurer Kinder hängt
von der Nutzung des Elterngelds ab!
Die Mütter zeigen euch den Weg.

Poster, GDR, 1950s

Carlos Winkow, 1938 | linotype.com

ABCDEFGH
FFKLMNOPQ
RSTUVWXYZ
abcdefghijklmn
opqrstuvwxyz
äöüß&%$?!.,:;*
1234567890

45 Point

Forsaking monastic tradition, twelve jovial friars
gave up their vocation for a questionable existence
on the flying trapeze.

16/25 Point

Brush & Swash

271

ABCDEFGH
IJKLMNOPQR
STUVWXYZ
abcdefghijklm
nopqrstuvwxyz
äöüßst $%?!.,:;
1234567890

48 Point

Forsaking monastic tradition, twelve
jovial friars gave up their vocation for a
questionable existence on the flying trapeze.

15/22 Point

ABCDEFGHIJ
KLMNOPQR
STUVWXYZ
abcdefghijklmn
opqrstuvwxyz
äöüß&$%@?!.,:;*
1234567890

44 Point

Forsaking monastic tradition, twelve jovial friars
gave up their vocation for a questionable existence
on the flying trapeze.

15/22 Point

Brush & Swash

ABCDEFGH
IJKLMNOPQ
RSTUVWXYZ
abcdefghijklmn
opqrstuvwxyz
äöüß&$%?!.,:;*
1234567890

40 Point

---

forsaking monastic tradition, twelve jovial
friars gave up their vocation for a questionable
existence on the flying trapeze.

14/25 Point

ABCDEFG
HIJKLMN
OPQRSTU
VWXYZ

abcdefghijklmn

opqrstuvwxyzäöüß

§&$%@?!.,:; *

1234567890

42 Point

Forsaking monastic tradition, twelve
jovial friars gave up their vocation for a
questionable existence on the flying trapeze.

18/25 Point

A B C D E F G
H I J K L M N
O P Q R S T U
V W X Y Z

abcdefghijklmnopqrst
uvwxyz&$%?!.,:;*
1234567890

43 Point

Forsaking monastic tradition, twelve jovial friars
gave up their vocation for a questionable existence
on the flying trapeze.

17/25 Point

ABCDEFG
HIJKLMN
OPQRSTU
VWXYZ

abcdefghijklmn

opqrstuvwxyzäöüß

&@$?!.,:;*

1234567890

48 Point

---

*F*orsaking monastic tradition, twelve jovial
friars gave up their vocation for a questionable
existence on the flying trapeze.

27/25 Point

Brush & Swash

ABCDEFG
HIJKLMN
OPQRSTU
VWXYZ

abcdefghijklmn

opqrstuvwxyz

äöüß&$%@?!.,:;*

1234567890

39 Point

---

*Forsaking monastic tradition, twelve
jovial friars gave up their vocation for a
questionable existence on the flying trapeze.*

16/25 Point

Imre Reiner, 1959 | linotype.com

ABCDEFG
HIJKLMN
OPQRSTU
VWXYZ

abcdefghijklmn
opqrstuvwxyz
&$%@?!.,:;*
1234567890

42 Point

Forsaking monastic tradition, twelve jovial friars
gave up their vocation for a questionable existence
on the flying trapeze.

16/25 Point

Luke Owens, 2004
fontspace.com | CD

A B C D E F G
H I J K L M N
O P Q R S T U
V W X Y Z
a b c d e f g h i j k l m n
o p q r s t u v w x y z ä ö ü ß
& § % ? ! . , ; : *
1 2 3 4 5 6 7 8 9 0

47 Point

Forsaking monastic tradition, twelve jovial
friars gave up their vocation for a questionable
existence on the flying trapeze.

20/25 Point

A B C D E F G
H I J K L M N
O P Q R S T U
V W X Y Z

abcdefghijklmnopqrstuvw
xyzäöü ß $%& ?!.,:; ❀
1234567890

32 Point

Forsaking monastic tradition, twelve jovial friars
gave up their vocation for a questionable existence
on the flying trapeze.

17/25 Point

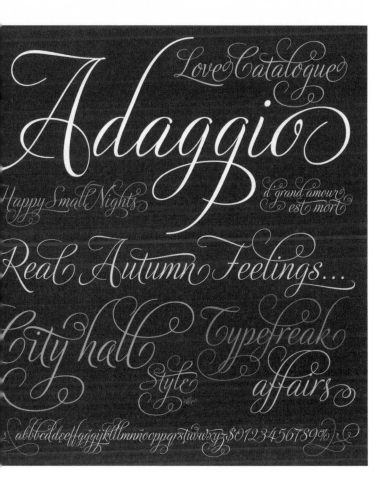

Adios script, Alejandro Paul, 2009

Campaign, Bill Thorburn, 1992

ABCDEFGH
IJKLMNOPQ
RSTUVWXYZ
abcdefghijklmn
opqrstuvwxyzäöüß
&$% @?!.,:;*
1234567890

50 Point

Forsaking monastic tradition, twelve jovial friars
gave up their vocation for a questionable existence
on the flying trapeze.

22/25 Point

Brush & Swash

A B C D E F G
H I J K L M N
O P Q R S T U
V W X Y Z

abcdefghijklmn
opqrstuvwxyzäöüß
$ & ?!.,:; *

1234567890

50 Point

Forsaking monastic tradition, twelve jovial friars
gave up their vocation for a questionable existence
on the flying trapeze.

20/25 Point

Book cover, Roberto de Vicq de Cumptich,
2009

Bloomington Arts
Movie Buffs
brainstorming session
Giant Alaskan King Crabs
Indian Pale Ale
Afternoon Schedule

Montague script, Stephen Rapp, 2009

ABCDEFGH
JJKLMNOPQ
RSTUVWXYZ

abcdefghijklmn

opqrstuvwxyzäöüß

$%&@?!.,.;*

1234567890

43 Point

Forsaking monastic tradition, twelve jovial friars
gave up their vocation for a questionable existence
on the flying trapeze.

23/24 Point

Brush & Swash

289

Derek Vogelpohl, 2008 | shyfoundry.com | CD

ABCDEZGH
IJKLMNOPQ
RSTUVWXYZ

abcdefghijklmnopqr
stuvwxyzäöü£$%?!.,:;
1234567890

60 Point

Forsaking monastic tradition, twelve jovial friars
gave up their vocation for a questionable existence
on the flying trapeze.

25/25 Point

ABCDEFGHIJ
KLMNOPQ
RSTUVWXYZ

abcdefghijklmn
opqrstuvwxyzäöü
$@&?!.,:;
1234567890

35 Point

Forsaking monastic tradition, twelve jovial
friars gave up their vocation for a questionable
existence on the flying trapeze.

14/25 Point

291

A Celebration...
...of work?

For our 1992 calendar we wanted to say something meaningful about the challenges of the coming year. There are a lot of buzz-words to choose from. Competitiveness. Globalization. Continuous improvement. Motherhood and maple syrup. But we think it can be said much more simply. The way to meet any big challenge is through plain old-fashioned hard work. Just getting down and doing it. And rather than drag out the soapbox, we'd prefer to communicate this simple message through a few strong images. After all, that's what our business is all about. So in the following pages we present portraits of 12 working people doing what they do best. As people have always done when it was most needed. This ain't exactly Hegelian metaphysics. All we're saying is, with the right initiative, energy and pride in achievement, we can make anything happen. And once we've got that licked, maybe we can try a new national anthem: "Heigh ho, heigh ho..."

Happy holidays and best wishes for a prosperous New Year
from all of us at Concrete.

CONCRETE
EM6-9908
THREE BRIGHT IDEAS EVERY DAY!

ABCDEFG
HIJKLMN
OPQRSTU
VWXYZ

abcdefghijklmnopqrstuvwxyz

äöüß § &-$@?!.,.:; *

1234567890

46 Point

Forsaking monastic tradition, twelve jovial friars
gave up their vocation for a questionable existence
on the flying trapeze.

21/25 Point

Brush & Swash

293

ABCDEFGHI

JKLMNOPQR

STUVWXYZ

abcdefghijklmn

opqrstuvwxyzäöüß

§&$@?!.,:;*

1234567890

38 Point

Forsaking monastic tradition, twelve jovial friars gave up their vocation for a questionable existence on the flying trapeze.

19/25 Point

Olivera Stojadinovic, 2001 | linotype.com

A B C D E F G
H I I K L M N
O P Q R S T U
V W X Y Z

abcdefghijklmn

opqrstuvwxyz

äöüß&@$?!.,.;*

1234567890

48 Point

Forsaking monastic tradition, twelve jovial friars
gave up their vocation for a questionable existence
on the flying trapeze.

19/25 Point

Brush & Swash

ABCDEFGHI
JKLMNOPQ
RSTUVWXYZ
abcdefghijklmno
pqrstuvwxyzäöüß
§&$@?!.,.:;*
1234567890

50 Point

Forsaking monastic tradition, twelve jovial friars
gave up their vocation for a questionable existence
on the flying trapeze.

17/25 Point

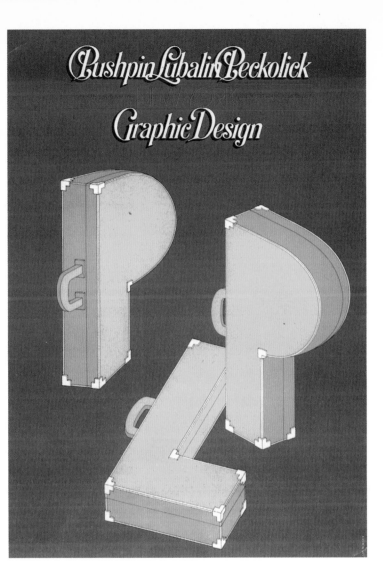

Poster, Alan Peckolick, 1984

Margaret
in Hollywood

A NOVEL

DARCY O'BRIEN

MORROW, AUTHOR OF MURDER IN LITTLE EGYPT

Brush & Swash

Book cover, Louise Fili, 1992

Soft Horizons, 1993 | abstractfonts.com | CD

ABCDEFG
HIJKLM
NOPQRST
UVWXYZ

abcdefghijklmn
opqrstuvwxyz
%$@&?!.,.; *
1234567890

35 Point

Forsaking monastic tradition, twelve jovial friars
gave up their vocation for a questionable existence on
the flying trapeze.

17/25 Point

Brush & Swash

299

ABCDEFGHIJK
LMNOPQRST
UVWXYZ
abcdefghijklmn
opqrstuvwxyz
&@?!.,:;*
1234567890

46 Point

Forsaking monastic tradition, twelve

jovial friars gave up their vocation for a

questionable existence on the flying trapeze.

14/25 Point

Phill Grimshaw, 1995 | linotype.com

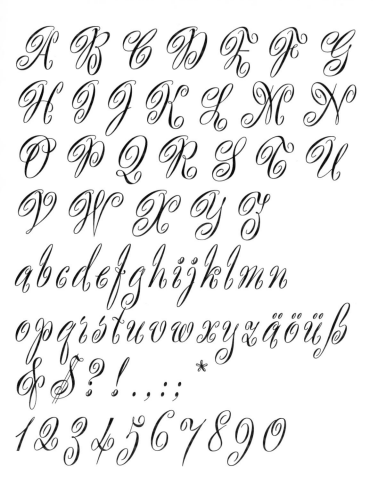

47 Point

Forsaking monastic tradition, twelve jovial
friars gave up their vocation for a questionable
existence on the flying trapeze.

22/25 Point

ABCDEFGHIJ

KLMNOPQR

STUVWXYZ

abcdefghijklmn

opqrstuvwxyz

äöüß&@$?!.,.;*

1234567890

30 Point

Forsaking monastic tradition, twelve jovial friars gave up their vocation for a questionable existence on the flying trapeze.

18/25 Point

Brush & Swash

ABCDEFG
HIJKLM
NOPQRST
UVWXYZ
abcdefghijklmn
opqrstuvwxyzäöüß
ſ&ſ@?!.,:;*
1234567890

36 Point

Forsaking monastic tradition, twelve jovial
friars gave up their vocation for a questionable
existence on the flying trapeze.

17/25 Point

Brush & Swash

303

TypeSETit–Robert E. Leuschke, 2004 | p22.com

ABCDEFG
HIJKLMN
OPQRSTU
VWXYZ

abcdefghijklmn

opqrstuvwxyzäöü ß

S&$?!.,.;*

1234567890

32 Point

Forsaking monastic tradition, twelve jovial friars gave up their vocation for a questionable existence on the flying trapeze.

15/25 Point

World Typeface Center

Poster, Tom Carnase, 1982

ABCDEFG
HIJKLMN
OPQRSTU
VWXYZ

abcdefghijklmn
opqrstuvwxyzäöüß
&$%@?!.,:;*
1234567890

40 Point

Forsaking monastic tradition, twelve jovial friars gave up their vocation for a questionable existence on the flying trapeze.

17/25 Point

A B C D E F G
H I J K L M N
O P Q R S T U
V W X Y Z

abcdefghijklmnopqrstuvwxyz

*äöüß § & @ $? ! . , . ; ***

1234567890

45 Point

---

*Forsaking monastic tradition, twelve jovial friars
gave up their vocation for a questionable existence
on the flying trapeze.*

25/25 Point

Brush & Swash

ABCDEFG
HIJKLMN
OPQRSTU
VWXYZ

a bcdefghijklmn
opqrstuvwxyz äöüß
&$%@?!.,.; ⚜
1234567890

30 Point

Forsa king mona suestra edition twelve
jodia Iria rs ga ve up their voca tion for a
questiona ble existence on the flying tra pez e.

15/25 Point

ABCDEFG
HIJKLMN
OPQRSTU
VWXYZ
abcdefghijklmn
opqrstuvwxyzäöüss
§&@$?!.,.;*
1234567890

44 Point

Forsaking monastic tradition, twelve jovial
friars gave up their vocation for a questionable
existence on the flying trapeze.

20/25 Point

Logos, student project,
Jason H. Wu (above), Betsy P. Tsai (below), 2009

ABCDEF
GHIJK
LMNOPQ
RSTUV
WXYZ

abcdefghijklmnopqrstuvwxyzäöüß

$@&?!.,.;*1234567890

25 Point

Forsaking monastic tradition, twelve jovial friars
gave up their vocation for a questionable existence
on the flying trapeze.

16/25 Point

Brush & Swash

A B C D E F

G H I J K

L M N O P

Q R S T U

V W X Y Z

abcdefghijklmn

opqrstuvwxyzäöüß

&$%@ ?!.,:; * 1234567890

34 Point

Forsaking monastic tradition, twelve
jovial friars gave up their vocation for a
questionable existence on the flying trapeze.

24/23 Point

T-shirt print, David Croy, 2009

With a Round Nib or a Felt Tip

We have centred our classification of the different script fonts primarily around writing implements, which shape the character of the script more profoundly than personality or epoch. By 'marker scripts' we mean fonts with a largely even width of line, as if written with a round redis nib, though all modern pens – from felt tips to biros – also have a roughly even line-width. Depending on which period they refer to, the scripts are strikingly different in terms of expressive character. Marker scripts can look similar to neat handwriting, and may be used to convey a similar authenticity – for notes, spontaneous annotations, and so on. But there is also a wide range of trendy applications for marker scripts, particularly as they are especially well suited to outlines and shadows.

Julius de Goede, 1999 | linotype.com

A B C D E F G H I J
K L M N O P Q R
S T U V W X Y Z
a b c d e f g h i j k l m n
o p q r s t u v w x y z
ä ö ü ß § $ & @ ? ! . , . ; *
1 2 3 4 5 6 7 8 9 0

52 Point

Forsaking monastic tradition, twelve jovial friars
gave up their vocation for a questionable existence
on the flying trapeze.

17/25 Point

Marker Scripts

320

MESATEX JAPAN FABRIC COLLECTION 2008

Poster, Gaku Ohsugi,
Yuriko Matsumura, 2008

Logotype, Richard Boynton, 2006

American Greetings Corporation, 1996 | dafont.com | → CD

ABCDEFGHI
JKLMNOPQR
STUVWXYZ

abcdefghijklmn
opqrstuvwxyzäöüß
&@%$?!.,.:;*

1234567890

50 Point

Forsaking monastic tradition, twelve jovial friars
gave up their vocation for a questionable existence
on the flying trapeze.

18/25 Point

Marker Scripts

ABCDEFGHIJ
KLMNOPQR
STUVWXYZ
abcdefghijklmnopq
rstuvwxyzäöüß
$§%&@?!.,.;*
1234567890

35 Point

Forsaking monastic tradition, twelve jovial friars
gave up their vocation for a questionable existence
on the flying trapeze.

14/25 Point

ABCDEFGHIJ
KLMNOPQRST
UVWXYZ
abcdefghijklmn
opqrstuvwxyz
äöüß££?!.,:;*
1234567890

42 Point

Forsaking monastic tradition, twelve jovial friars
gave up their vocation for a questionable existence
on the flying trapeze.

17/25 Point

ABCDEFGHI
JKLMNOPQR
STUVWXYZ
abcdefghijklmn
opqrstuvwxyz
äöüß&@%$?!.,:;*
1234567890

47 Point

Forsaking monastic tradition, twelve
jovial friars gave up their vocation for a
questionable existence on the flying trapeze.

16/25 Point

Poster, Armin Lindauer, 1996

ABCDEFGHIJ
KLMNOPQR
STUUWXYZ
abcdefghijklmn
opqrstuvwxyzäöüß
&$§%@?!.,.;*
1234567890

43 Point

Forsaking monastic tradition, twelve jovial friars
gave up their vocation for a questionable existence
on the flying trapeze.

23/25 Point

Linotype Design Studio, 2003 | linotype.com

A B C D E F G
H I J K L M N
O P Q R S T
U V W X Y Z

abcdefghijklmn
opqrstuvwxyzäöüß
&$§%@?!.,:;*
1234567890

30 Point

Forsaking monastic tradition, twelve jovial
friars gave up their vocation for a questionable
existence on the flying trapeze.

15/25 Point

Ko Sliggers, 2008 | dutchfonts.de

ABCDEFGHIJ
KLMNOPQR
STUVWXYZ
abcdefghijk
lmnopqrstu
vwxyzäöüß
&@$?!.,:;*
1234567890

44 Point

Forsaking monastic tradition, twelve
jovial friars gave up their vocation for a
questionable existence on the flying trapeze.

12/25 Point

Marker Scripts

ABCDEFGH
IJKLMNOPQR
STUVWXYZ

abcdefghijklmn
opqrstuvwxyz
$%¢ ?!.,:;*
1234567890

41 Point

Forsaking monastic tradition, twelve
jovial friars gave up their vocation for a
questionable existence on the flying trapeze.

14/25 Point

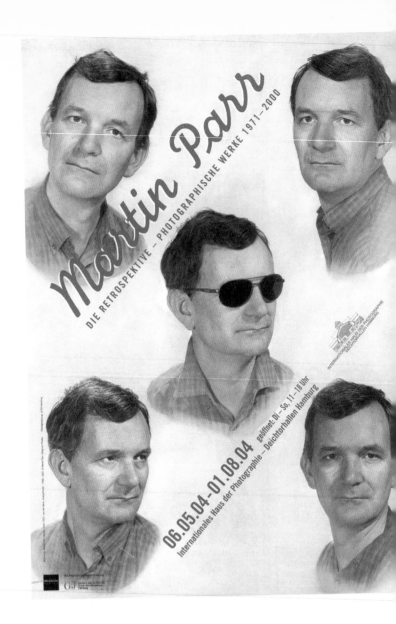

Poster, Torsten Krüger, Wolfgang Greter, 2004

ABCDEFGH
IJKLMNOPQ
RSTUVWXYZ
abcdefghijklmn
opqrstuvwxyz
&?!.,.:;"*
1234567890

32 Point

Forsaking monastic tradition, twelve jovial

friars gave up their vocation for a questionable

existence on the flying trapeze.

10/25 Point

ABCDEFGHIJ
KLMNOPQR
STUVWXYZ
abcdefghijklm
nopqrstuvwxyz
äöüß&@$?!.,:;*
1234567890

37 Point

Forsaking monastic tradition, twelve

jovial friars gave up their vocation for a

questionable existence on the flying trapeze.

12/25 Point

Poster, Tadanori Yokoo, 1989

ABCDEFGH
IJKLMNOPQ
RSTUVWXYZ
abcdefghijklmn
opqrstuvwxyz
äöüß§$@&?!.,:;*
1234567890

42 Point

Forsaking monastic tradition, twelve jovial friars gave up their vocation for a questionable existence on the flying trapeze.

15/25 Point

Andrij Shevchenko, 2006 | myfonts.com

ABCDEFG
HIJKLMN
OPQRSTU
VWXYZ
abcdefghijklmn
opqrstuvwxyz
$§%&@?!.,:;*
1234567890

41 Point

Forsaking monastic tradition, twelve
jovial friars gave up their vocation for a
questionable existence on the flying trapeze.

16/25 Point

ABCDEFGH IJKLMNOPQ RSTUVWXYZ

abcdefghijklmn

opqrstuvwxyz

äöüßſs@&?!.,.:;*

1234567890

45 Point

Forsaking monastic tradition, twelve jovial friars gave up their vocation for a questionable existence on the flying trapeze.

19/25 Point

ABCDEFGH
IJKLMNOPQ
RSTUVWXYZ
abcdefghijklmn
opqrstuvwxyzäöüß
$§%& @?!.,.; *
1234567890

4 Point

Forsaking monastic tradition, twelve jovial friars
gave up their vocation for a questionable existence
on the flying trapeze.

9/25 Point

Marker Scripts

ABCDEFGH
IJKLMNOPQR
STUVWXYZ
abcdefghijklmn
opqrstuvwxyz
äöüß& $?!.,:;*
1234567890

47 Point

Forsaking monastic tradition, twelve jovial friars gave up their vocation for a questionable existence on the flying trapeze.

17/25 Point

Book cover, Richard Moore, 1983

Book cover, Fritz von Valtier, 1932

Nick Curtis, 2000 | nicksfonts.com | CD

ABCDEFGHIJ
KLMNOPQR
STUVWXYZ
abcdefghijklmn
opqrstuvwxyz
äöüß&$?!.,.:;
1234567890

47 Point

Forsaking monastic tradition, twelve
jovial friars gave up their vocation for a
questionable existence on the flying trapeze.

19/25 Point

Marker Scripts

343

ABCDEFGH
IJKLMNOPQ
RSTUVWXYZ
abcdefghijklmn
opqrstuvwxyzäöüß
fifl$%&?!.,:; *
1234567890

46 Point

Forsaking monastic tradition, twelve jovial friars gave up their vocation for a questionable existence on the flying trapeze.

17/25 Point

ABCDEFGHI
JKLMNOPQR
STUVWXYZ

abcdefghijklmn
opqrstuvwxyzäöüß
&@$?!.,.;*
1234567890

47 Point

Forsaking monastic tradition, twelve jovial friars
gave up their vocation for a questionable existence
on the flying trapeze.

19/25 Point

Marker Scripts

345

ABCDEFGH
IJKLMNOPQ
RSTUVWXYZ

abcdefghijklmn
opqrstuvwxyzäöüss
&%@?!.,:;*
1234567890

42 Point

Forsaking monastic tradition, twelve jovial friars
gave up their vocation for a questionable existence
on the flying trapeze.

20/25 Point

Marker Scripts

346

Poster, Ultrabazar – Märt Infanger, 2005

ABCDEFGHI
JKLMNOPQR
STUVWXYZ

abcdefghijklmn

opqrstuvwxyzäöüß

$%&?!.,:; *

1234567890

40 Point

Forsaking monastic tradition, twelve jovial friars
gave up their vocation for a questionable existence
on the flying trapeze.

18/25 Point

A B C D E F G H I J
K L M N O P Q R
S T U V W X Y Z

abcdefghijklmn
opqrstuvwxyzäöüß
$§%&@?!.,:;*
1234567890

56 Point

Forsaking monastic tradition, twelve jovial friars
gave up their vocation for a questionable existence
on the flying trapeze.

20/25 Point

Packaging, Michael Strassburger, 1996

Diane Dipiazza, 2006 | girlswhowearglasses.com | CD

ABCDEFGH
IgKLMNOPQ
RSTUVWXYZ

abcdefghijklmn

opqrstuvwxyz

&?!.,:;*●

1234567890

37 Point

Forsaking monastic tradition, twelve jovial friars
gave up their vocation for a questionable existence
on the flying trapeze.

15/25 Point

Marker Scripts

Max R. Kaufmann, 1936 | linotype.com

ABCDEFGHIJ
KLMNOPQR
STUVWXYZ

abcdefghijklmn
opqrstuvwxyzäöüß
$%§&@?.,:;*
1234567890

37 Point

Forsaking monastic tradition, twelve
jovial friars gave up their vocation for a
questionable existence on the flying trapeze.

17/25 Point

ABCDEFGH
IJKLMNOPQ
RSTUVWXYZ
abcdefghijklmn
opqrstuvwxyzäöüß
&$%@?!.,.;*
1234567890

45 Point

Forsaking monastic tradition, twelve jovial friars
gave up their vocation for a questionable existence
on the flying trapeze.

17/25 Point

ABCDEFG
HIJKLMN
OPQRSTU
VWXYZ

abcdefghijklmn

opqrstuvwxyzäöüß

$&?!.,:;*

1234567890

38 Point

Forsaking monastic tradition, twelve
jovial friars gave up their vocation for a
questionable existence on the flying trapeze.

16/25 Point

Advertisement, Morgan Daniels, 1997

ABCDEFG
HIJKLMN
OPQRSTU
VWXYZ
abcdefghijklmn
opqrstuvwxyz
&?!.,:;
1234567890

49 Point

Forsaking monastic tradition, twelve

jovial friars gave up their vocation for a

questionable existence on the flying trapeze.

16/25 Point

Sharkshock Productions, 2000 | sharkshock.uni.cc | CD

A B C D E F G
H I J K L M N
O P Q R S T U
V W X Y Z
a b c d e f g h i j k l m n
o p q r s t u v w x y z
$? ! . . , . ;
1 2 3 4 5 6 7 8 9 0

40 Point

Forsaking monastic tradition, twelve
jovial friars gave up their vocation for a
questionable existence on the flying trapeze.

15/25 Point

Marker Scripts

357

ABCDEFGH
IJKLMNOPQ
RSTUVWXYZ

abcdefghijklmn

opqrstuvwxyzäöüß

&$@?!.,:; 1234567890

40 Point

Forsaking monastic tradition, twelve jovial friars
gave up their vocation for a questionable existence
on the flying trapeze.

17/25 Point

American Greetings Corporation, 1996 | abstractfonts.com | CD

$$ABCDEFGHI$$

$$JKLMNOPQ$$

$$RSTUVWXYZ$$

abcdefghijklmn

opqrstuvwxyzäöüß

$&@?!.,.;*

1234567890

44 Point

Forsaking monastic tradition, twelve jovial friars
gave up their vocation for a questionable existence
on the flying trapeze.

18/25 Point

Marker Scripts

359

Nick Curtis, 2000 | nicksfonts.com | CD

ABCDEFGHIJ
KLMNOPQR
STUVWXYZ
abcdefghijklmn
opqrstuvwxyz
äöüß&@$?!.,:;*
1234567890

37 Point

Forsaking monastic tradition, twelve jovial
friars gave up their vocation for a questionable
existence on the flying trapeze.

14/25 Point

Brochure, Louise Fili, Jessica Hische, 2009

ABCDEFGH
IJKLMNOPQ
RSTUVWXYZ
abcdefghijklmn
opqrstuvwxyz
äöüß$%&@?!.,.;*
1234567890

34 Point

Forsaking monastic tradition, twelve
jovial friars gave up their vocation for a
questionable existence on the flying trapeze.

14/25 Point

Marker Scripts

Richard William Mueller, 1993 | moorstation.org | CD

ABCDEFGH
IJKLMNOPQR
STUVWXYZ

abcdefghijklmn
opqrstuvwxyz
äöüßß$&@?!.,:;*
1234567890

48 Point

Forsaking monastic tradition, twelve

jovial friars gave up their vocation for a

questionable existence on the flying trapeze.

16/25 Point

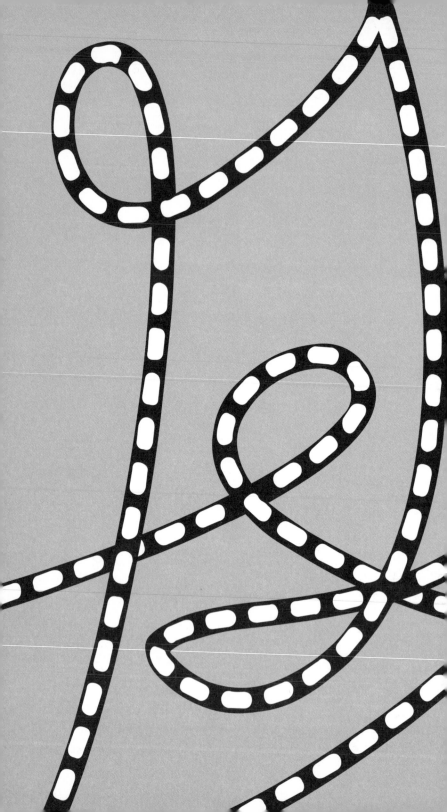

200 Years of Teaching Writing

The way you are taught to write in school has a lifelong effect on your handwriting. A whole generation of Germans now well into their eighties had to adapt twice over the years, from *Lateinischer Ausgangsschrift* (a standard cursive) to Sütterlin and back again. Ways of teaching the alphabet to primary-school children also varied significantly from country to country, engendering an array of different styles of school handwriting. This chapter takes us on a historical journey from Sütterlin (page 376) to *Lateinischer Ausgangsschrift* ('Schulschrift OTB', page 377) to simplified *Ausgangsschrift* ('Schulschrift OTA', page 379). Such scripts are mainly used in books designed to teach children how to read, although many people equally recommend standard roman or sans serif faces for young readers.

Old-style school scripts are most effective in creating a retro design that evokes the past, or for adaptive typography. A closer look at individual characters will reveal whether the script comes from Switzerland, France or the United States.

ABCDEFGHIJ
KLMNOPQR
STUVWXYZ

abcdefghijklmn
opqrstuvwxyz

äöüß§$%&?!.,:;*

1234567890

43 Point

Forporking monoftic tradition, tradion jovial friend
gown ity thrir vocation for a quiftionable riftmen
on the flying trograze.

16/25 Point

Book cover, O. Maier Verlag, 1941

Book cover, Deutsche Maizena-Gesellschaft
[a German manufacturer of corn starch
products], Hamburg, c. 1925

Book cover, Publishing House of the
German Dental Association, Berlin, 1937

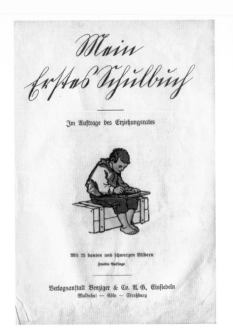

Mein Erstes Schulbuch

Im Auftrage des Erziehungsrates

Mit 75 bunten und schwarzen Bildern

Zweite Auflage

Verlagsanstalt Benziger & Co. A. G., Einsiedeln
Waldshut — Köln — Straßburg

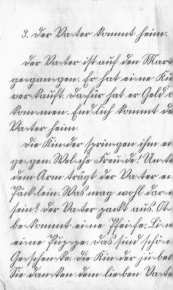

3. Der Vater kommt heim.

Der Vater ist auf dem Markt gegangen. Er hat eine Kuh verkauft. Dafür hat er Geld bekommen. Endlich kommt der Vater heim.

Die Kinder springen ihm entgegen. Welche Freude! Unterm Arm trägt der Vater etwas. Was mag wohl das sein? Der Vater zeigt es. Oh, da kommt eine Schachtel. Ei, eine Spitze. Das sind schöne Geschenke. Die Kinder jubeln. Sie danken dem lieben Vater.

sch, schön,

schau, frisch, schnell,
wasche dich rasch!

na-sche ja nicht, das wä-re bö-se!

st, ste, ist,

Stiel, selbst,

bist du dur-stig? ste-he recht fest!

ß, naß,

iß, laß, daß, grüß

man muß stets flei-ßig sein, ge-w
iß nur mä-ßig und nicht zu he

au, äu

schau, blau, m

träu-men, schäu-men, grau, bl
glau-be mir doch, es läu-tet sch

Schulb. 1

Mein Erstes Schulbuch [My First Schoolbook], Switzerland, 1920

Derek Vogelpohl, 2008 | shyfoundry.com | CD

A B L V E F G H I J

K L M N O P Q R

S T U V W X Y Z

a b c d e f g h i j k l m n

o p q r s t u v w x y z ä ö ü ß

& ? ! . , . , ; 1 2 3 4 5 6 7 8 9 0

43 Point

Forsaking monastic tradition, wanton jovial friars
gave up their vocation for a questionable regiment
on the flying trapeze.

17/25 Point

School Scripts

373

abcdefghiklm
nopqrɛsßtuʋn
?, xyz !.
ABCDEFGG
HIKLMNO
PQRSTU
WXYZ
1234567890

'Roundhand', Malerschule Zimmermann
[Zimmermann School of Painting],
Mannheim-Neckarau, c. 1930

1234567890

'German handwriting', Malerschule
Zimmermann [Zimmermann School of
Painting], Mannheim-Neckarau, *c.* 1930

$\mathcal{A}$ $\mathcal{B}$ $\mathcal{C}$ $\mathcal{D}$ $\mathcal{EF}$ $\mathcal{G}$ $\mathcal{H}$ $\mathcal{IJ}$

$\mathcal{K}$ $\mathcal{L}$ $\mathcal{M}$ $\mathcal{N}$ $\mathcal{O}$ $\mathcal{P}$ $\mathcal{Q}$ $\mathcal{R}$

$\mathcal{S}$ $\mathcal{T}$ $\mathcal{U}$ $\mathcal{V}$ $\mathcal{W}$ $\mathcal{X}$ $\mathcal{Y}$ $\mathcal{Z}$

a b c d e f g h i j k

l m n o p q r s t u

v w x y z

6 % & ⓐ ? ! . , : ; *

1 2 3 4 5 6 7 8 9 0

40 Point

---

forsaking monastic tradition, trenton jovial

frisky gave up this donation for a questionable

neighbor on the flying trapeze.

10/25 Point

Just van Rossum, 1991 | fontshop.com

A B C D E F G H I J
K L M N O P Q R
S T U V W X Y Z
a b c d e f g h i j k l m n o p q
r s t u v w x y z ä ö ü ß
a b c d e f g h i j k l m n o p q
r s t u v w x y z ä ö ü ß
1 2 3 4 5 6 7 8 9 0

44 Point

Forsaking monastic tradition, twelve
jovial friars gave up their vocation for a
questionable existence on the flying trapeze.

18/25 Point

ABCDEFGHIJKL
MNOPQRST
UVWXYZ

a b c d e f g h i j k
l m n o p q r s ß t u
v w x y z

1 2 3 4 5 6 7 8 9 0

Vom Ministerium für Volksbildung der Deutschen Demokratischen Republik
als Schulbuch bestätigt

16. Auflage · Ausgabe 1970
Lizenz Nr. 203 · 1000/83 (UN 100261–16)
LSV 0681
Redaktion: Dorothea Türk, Irmgard Kinitz
Grafische Gestaltung: Renate Tost
Printed in the German Democratic Republic
Gesamtherstellung: VEB Hermes, Halle
Redaktionsschluß: 20. April 1983
Bestell-Nr. 730 144 1

Kurzwort: 100261 Schreib-Ueb.H3,Kl2
Schulpreis DDR 0,20

School Scripts

Back of a school notebook, *c.* 1983

378

ABCDEFGHIJ
KLMNOPQR
STUVWXYZ
abcdefghijklmn
opqrstuvwxyzäöüß
abcdefghijklmn
opqrstuvwxyzäöüß
1234567890

40 Point

Forsaking monastic tradition, twelve jovial
friars gave up their vocation for a questionable
existence on the flying trapeze.

16/25 Point

ABCDEFGHIJ
KLMNOPQR
STUVWXYZ
abcdefghijklmn
opqrstuvwxyz
äöüß?!.,:;
1234567890

43 Point

Forsaking monastic tradition, twelve
jovial friars gave up their vocation for a
questionable existence on the flying trapeze.

15/25 Point

Jess Latham, 2007 | bvfonts.com | CD

ABCDEFGHI
JKLMNOPQR
STUVWXYZ
abcdefghijklmn
opqrstuvwxyzäöüß
§%&@?!.,:;*
1234567890

32 Point

Forsaking monastic tradition, twelve
jovial friars gave up their vocation for a
questionable existence on the flying trapeze.

23/25 Point

ABCDEFG
HIJKLMN
OPQRSTU
VWXYZ
abcdefghijklmn
opqrstuvwxyz
äöüßß§&@?!.,.;
1234567890

40 Point

Forsaking monastic tradition, twelve jovial friars gave up their vocation for a questionable existence on the flying trapeze.

14/25 Point

Jean Claude Gineau | urbanfonts.com | CD

A B C D E F G H I J

K L M N O P Q R

S T U V W X Y Z

abcdefghijklmn

opqrstuvwxyz

&%@?!.,.;*

1234567890

37 Point

Forsaking monastic tradition, twelve jovial
friars gave up their vocation for a questionable
existence on the flying trapeze.

15/25 Point

ABCDEFG
HIJKLMN
OPQRSTU
VWXYZ

abcdefghijklmn
opqrstuvwxyz
äöüß&$@?!.,.;*
1234567890

40 Point

Forsaking monastic tradition, twelve
jovial friars gave up their vocation for a
questionable existence on the flying trapeze.

16/25 Point

ABCDEFGHIJ
KLMNOPQR
STUVWXYZ

abcdefghijklmn
opqrstuvwxyz
§&@?! .,.:; *
1234567890

46 Point

Forsaking monastic tradition, twelve
jovial friars gave up their vocation for a
questionable existence on the flying trapeze.

16/25 Point

School Scripts

ABCDEFG
HIJKLMN
OPQRSTU
VWXYZ
abcdefghijklmn
opqrstuvwxyz
$%&@?!.,.;❦
1234567890

29 Point

Forsaking monastic tradition, twelve jovial
friars gave up their vocation for a questionable
existence on the flying trapeze.

10/25 Point

ABCDEFGH

IJKLMNOPQ

RSTUVWXYZ

abcdefghijklmn

opqrstuvwxyz

äöüß&$@?!.,;*

1234567890

37 Point

Forsaking monastic tradition, twelve
jovial friars gave up their vocation for a
questionable existence on the flying trapeze.

12/25 Point

School Scripts

From Punk to arabic

The wealth of variety among script fonts is astonishing; designing fonts and digitizing idiosyncratic letters has become an appealing discipline for many designers.

Inspired by 1950s car-bumper lettering or neon signs, these scripts are not exactly 'handwriting', but, as with script fonts, all the letters are joined up. Elements drawn from street art and graffiti are often central to their style: these typefaces take their cue from script fonts in the public sphere. Existing scripts are defaced, morphed or given a 'used look' with filters. Extra swashes and flourishes are added, or attributes of foreign scripts like Cyrillic, Arabic or Chinese are incorporated into the Latin alphabet. There are virtually no limits on the imagination, since neither readability nor overall harmony within the font are a factor. Such decorative typefaces often serve for single headlines or logos. Dozens of them are produced every day, and are circulated via font platforms for enthusiasts to use and enjoy.

ABCDEFGHIJK
LMNOPQR
STUVWXYZ

abcdefghijklmn
opqrstuvwxyz
àäüßø@s?!.,p
1234567890

43 Point

forsaking monastic tradition, twelve jovial friars
gave up their vocation for a questionable
existence on the flying trapeze.

15/25 Point

Alfredo Häberli
Design Development
Surround things

Museum für Gestaltung
Zürich

27.6.–21.9.2008

www.museum-gestaltung.ch

Poster, Stefanie Häberli-Bachmann, 2008

ABCDEFGHI
JKLMNOPQR
STUVWXYZ
abcdefghijklmn
opqrstuvwxyz
&@§%$?!)(„·ı:¡*
1234567890

41 Point

Forsaking monastic tradition, twelve
jovial friars gave up their vocation for a
questionable existence on the flying trapeze.

13/25 Point

Masato Shimojima, 1999 | urbanfonts.com | CD

ABCDEFGH
IJKLMNOPQ
RSTUVUWXYZ

abcdeßghijklmn
opqrstuvwxyz
äöüß&@$?!.,:;*
1234567890

45 Point

Forsaking monastic tradition, twelve jovial Briars
gave up their vocation for a questionable existence
on the flying trapeze.

14/25 Point

Decorative and Freestyle

ABCDEFG
HIJKLMN
OPQRST
UVWXYZ

abcdefg
hijklmn
opqrstu
vwxyzäöüß
$&@$?!.,:;*
1234567890

28 Point

Forsaking monastic tradition,
twelve jovial friars gave up
their vocation for a questionable
existence on the flying trapeze.

9/17 Point

Vehicle lettering, 1950s

Decorative and Freestyle

Nick Curtis, 1999 | nicksfonts.com | CD

A B C D E F G H
I J K L M N O P Q R
S T U V W X Y Z

abcdefghijk
lmnopqrstu
vwxyzäöüß
&@%$?!.,:;*
1234567890

44 Point

Forsaking monastic tradition, twelve
jovial friars gave up their vocation for a
questionable existence on the flying trapeze

15/25 Point

$ABCDEFG$

$HIJKLM$

$NOPQRST$

$UVWXYZ$

abcdefghijklmn

opqrstuvwxyz

äöüß&$@?!.,.;*

1234567890

30 Point

Forsaking monastic tradition, twelve

jovial friars gave up their vocation for a

questionable existence on the flying trapeze.

9.5/25 Point

abcdefgh
ijklmnopqr
stuvwxyz
abcdefghij
klmnopqrstu
vwxyzaäöüß
& at $?!.,:;*
1234567890

44 Point

forsaking monastic tradition, twelve

jovial friars gave up their vocation for a

questionable existence on the flying trapeze.

11.5/ 25 Point

Nick Curtis, 2002 | nicksfonts.com | CD

ABCDEFGH
IJKLMNOPQ
RSTUVWXYZ
abcdefghijklmn
opqrstuvwxyz
äöüß&@$?!.,:;*
1234567890

42 Point

Forsaking monastic tradition, twelve
jovial friars gave up their vocation for a
questionable existence on the flying trapeze

14/25 Point

Poster, Christof Nardin,
Thomas Geisler, 2006

Decorative and Freestyle

ABCDEFG
HIJKLMN
OPQRSTU
VWXYZ
abcdefghijklmn
opqrstuvwxyz
äüöß &$ @ ?!.,.;*
1234567890

48 Point

Forsaking monastic tradition, twelve jovial friars
gave up their vocation for a questionable existence
on the flying trapeze.

16/25 Point

Brian Kent | aenigmafonts.com | CD

ABCDEFGH
IJKLMNOPQ
RSTUVWXYZ
abcdefghijk
lmnopqrstu
vwxyz
£$@?!.,.;¨*
1234567890

38 Point

Forsaking monastic tradition, twelve jovial

friars gave up their vocation for a

questionable existence on the flying trapeze.

11/25 Point

K. Steens, 1999 | bold-design.com | CD

ABCDEFGHIJ

KLMNOPQR

STUVWXYZ

abcdefghijklmno

pqrstuvwxyzäöüß

&%@?!,.:; *Velocette*

1234567890

48 Point

Forsaking monastic tradition, twelve jovial
friars gave up their vocation for a questionable
existence on the flying trapeze.

8/25 Point

Decorative and Freestyle

407

A B C D E F G
H I J K L M N
O P Q R S T
U V W X Y Z
abcdefghijklmn
opqrstuvwxyz
äöüß&$% @ ?!.,;:*
1234567890

26 Point

---

*Forsaking monastic tradition, twelve
jovial friars gave up their vocation for a
questionable existence on the flying trapeze.*

13/23 Point

Zero (herz)
Trip-hop Tribute
www.myspace.com/zeroherz
www.myspace.com/triphopproject
Missy Bar
250, Mont-Royal Est
www.missybar.com
7 avril 21 h
P.S.

A B C D E F G
H I J K L M N
O P Q R S T U
V W X Y Z
abcdefghijklmn
opqrstuvwxyz
$ % & @ ? ! . , . ; *
1 2 3 4 5 6 7 8 9 0

36 Point

Forsaking monastic tradition, twelve jovial friars gave up their vocation for a questionable existence on the flying trapeze.

20/25 Point

Douglas Vitkauskas | vtks.com.br | CD

ABCDEFGHI
JKLMNOPQR
STUVWXYZ

abcdefghijklmn
opqrstuvwxyz
$@?!.,:;
1234567890

50 Point

Forsaking monastic tradition, twelve
jovial friars gave up their vocation for a
questionable existence on the flying trapeze.

1/25 Point

Decorative and Freestyle

411

A B C D E F G

H I J K L M

N O P Q R S T

U V W X Y Z

abcdefghijklmnopqrstuvwxyz

äöü $%&@ !,.:;

1234567890

18 Point

Forsaking monastic tradition, twelve jovial friars gave up their vocation for a questionable existence on the flying trapeze.

13/25 Point

43 Point

Forsaking monastic tradition, twelve jovial
friars gave up their vocation for a questionable
existence on the flying trapeze.

20/25 Point

Decorative and Freestyle

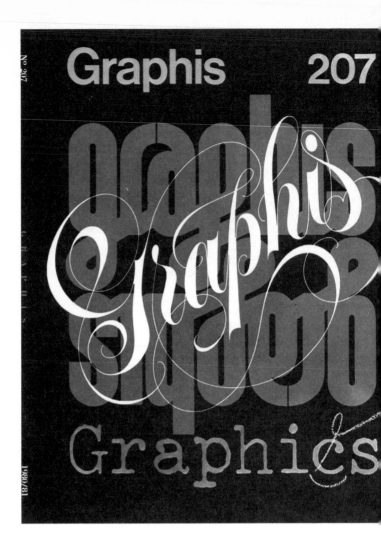

Magazine cover, Alan Peckolick, Ernie Smith,
Tony DiSpigna, 1982

A B C D E F
G H I J K L M
N O P Q R S T
U V W X Y Z
abcdefghijklmn
opqrstuvwxyzäöüß
& S % @ ?!.,.:; *
1234567890

52 Point

Forsaking monastic tradition, twelve jovial friars
gave up their vocation for a questionable existence
on the flying trapeze.

26/25 Point

ABCDEFGHI

JKLMNOPQR

STUVWXYZ

abcdefghijklmn

opqrstuvwxyz

&$?!.,:;

1234567890

40 Point

Forsaking monastic tradition, twelve jovial friars gave up their vocation for a questionable existence on the flying trapeze.

15/25 Point

ABCDEFGH
IJKLMNOPQ
RSTUVWXYZ
abcdefghijklmn
opqrstuvwxyz
äöüß&"
1234567890

42 Point

Forsaking monastic tradition, twelve
jovial friars gave up their vocation for a
questionable existence on the flying trapeze

15/25 Point

Decorative and Freestyle

ABCDEFG
HIJKLM
NOPQRST
UVWXYZ
abcdefghijklmn
opqrstuvwxyzäöüß
&$C@?!.,.;*
1234567890

44 Point

Forsaking monastic tradition, twelve jovial friars gave up their vocation for a questionable existence on the flying trapeze.

18/25 Point

A B C D E F
G H I J K L M
N O P Q R S T
U V W X Y Z
abcdefghijklmn
opqrstuvwxyzäöüß
&$?!.,:;
1234567890

45 Point

Forsaking monastic tradition, twelve jovial friars
gave up their vocation for a questionable existence
on the flying trapeze.

19/25 Point

36 Point

Forsaking monastic tradition, twelve jovial friars gave up their vocation for a questionable existence on the flying trapeze.

18/25 Point

Decorative and Freestyle

TypeSETit–Robert E. Leuschke, 2004 | p22.com

A B C D E F G
H I J K L M N
O P Q R S T U
V W X Y Z

abcdefghijklmn

opqrstuvwxyz äöü ß fi fl

$ ‰ $ @ & ? ! . , . ; *

1 2 3 4 5 6 7 8 9 0

49 Point

Forsaking monastic tradition, twelve jovial friars
gave up their vocation for a questionable existence on
the flying trapeze.

24/25 Point

Dieter Steffmann, 2001 | steffmann.de | CD

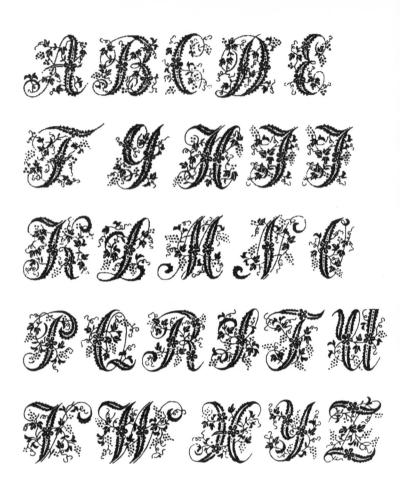

58 Point

FORMERLY MONASTIC TRADITION
TWELVE ITALIAN FRIARS GAVE UP
THEIR VOCATION FOR A QUESTIONABLE
EXISTENCE OF THE FLYING TRAPEZE

12/19 Point

Dan X. Solo, 2000 | abstractfonts.com | CD

A B C D E F G
H I J K L M N
O P Q R S T U
V W X Y Z
a b c d e f g h i j k l m n
o p q r s t u v w x y z
ä ö ü ß & @ $? ! . , : ; *
1 2 3 4 5 6 7 8 9 0

40 Point

Forsaking monastic tradition, twelve jovial friars
gave up their vocation for a questionable existence
on the flying trapeze.

18/25 Point

Decorative and Freestyle

53 Point

Forsaking monastic tradition, twelve jovial friars gave up their vocation for a questionable existence on the flying trapeze.

26/25 Point

Ray Larabie, 1999 | larabiefonts.com | CD

ABCDEFGH
IJKZMNOPZ
RSTUVWXYZ
abcdefghijklmn
opqrstuvwxyzäöüß
£%$@?!.,:;*
1234567890

44 Point

Forsaking monastic tradition, twelve jovial friars
gave up their vocation for a questionable existence on
the flying trapeze.

22/25 Point

Decorative and Freestyle

425

Maximiliano Sproviero, 2007 | myfonts.com

abcdergghijj
klmnopqr
stuvwxyz

abcdefghijhlmn

opgrstuvwxyz

$@?!.,:1234567890

23 Point

Forsaking monastic tradition, twelve
jovial friars gave up their vocation for a
questionable existence on the flying trapeze.

12/25 Point

ABCDEFGH
IJKLMNOPQ
RSTUVWXYZ

abcdefghijklmnopqrstuvwxyz

äöü & % @ ? ! . , : ; *

1234567890

18 Point

Forsaking monastic tradition, twelve jovial friars gave
up their vocation for a questionable existence on
the flying trapeze.

10/30 Point

Decorative and Freestyle

427

ABCDEFGH
IJKLMNOPQR
STUVWXYZ
abcdefghijklmn
opqrstuvwxyz
äöüß&%$?!.,:; ✳
1234567890

40 Point

Forsaking monastic tradition, twelve
jovial friars gave up their vocation for a
questionable existence on the flying trapeze.

17.5/25 Point

Poster, Nina Pagalies, 1951

ABCDEFGH
IJKLMNOPQR
STUVWXYZ

ABCDEFGHIJk LMN
OPQRSTUVWXYZÄÖÜß
$ZE@@?!.,;:*
1234567890

39 Point

Forsaking monastic tradition, twelve
jovial friars gave up their vocation for a
questionable existence on the flying trapeze.

13/25 Point

ABCDEFGHIJ
KLMNOPQR
STUVWXYZ
abcdefghijklmn
opqrstuvwxyz
äöü$%&@?!.,;:*
1234567890

55 Point

Forsaking monastic tradition, twelve jovial friars
gave up their vocation for a questionable existence
on the flying trapeze.

20/25 Point

Decorative and Freestyle

ABCDEFGHIJ
KLMNOPQR
STUVWXYZ
abcdefghijk
lmnopqrstu
vwxyz
@?!.,:;1234567890

40 Point

Forsaking monastic tradition, twelve
jovial friars gave up their vocation for a
questionable existence on the flying trapeze.

13/25 Point

432

A B C D E F
G H I J K L M N
O P Q R S T
U V W X Y Z
a b c d e f g h i j k l m n
o p q r s t u v w x y z ä ö ü ß
& % $ @ ? ! . , : ; *
1 2 3 4 5 6 7 8 9 0

7 Point

Forsaking monastic tradition, twelve
ovial friars gave up their vocation for a
questionable existence on the flying trapeze.

4/25 Point

"Imagine
that you have before you a
flagon of wine. You may choose
your own favorite vintage for this imagi-
nary demonstration, so that it be a deep
shimmering crimson in your colour. You have
two goblets before you. One is of solid gold,
wrought in the most exquisite patterns. The
other is of crystal-clear glass, thin as a bubble,
and as transparent. Pour and drink; and
according to your choice of goblet, I
shall know whether or not you are
a connoisseur of wine..."

— Beatrice

Specimen sheet, Olivera Stojadinovic, 2001

ABCDEFGHIJ
KLMNOPQR
STUVWXYZ
abcdefghijklmn
opqrstuvwxyzäöüß
§&@$?!.,.;*
1234567890

45 Point

Forsaking monastic tradition, twelve jovial friars
gave up their vocation for a questionable existence
on the flying trapeze.

20/25 Point

ABCDEFGHIJ
KLMNOPQR
STUVWXYZ
abcdefghijklmno
pqrstuvwxyzäöüß
$%&@?!.,:;*
1234567890

52 Point

Forsaking monastic tradition, twelve jovial friars
gave up their vocation for a questionable existence
on the flying trapeze.

23/25 Point

Panhandler

David Buck, 2003 | sparkytype.com

ABCDEFGHIJ
KLMNOPQR
STUVWXYZ

abcdefghijklmnopqrstuvwxyz

äöüß&%§@?!.,:;*

1234567890

40 Point

Forsaking monastic tradition, twelve jovial
friars gave up their vocation for a questionable
existence on the flying trapeze.

22/24 Point

ABCDEFGHIJKLMN
OPQRSTUVWXYZ
abcdefghijklmn
opqrstuvwxyzäöüß
§&$@?!.,:;*
1234567890

51 Point

Forsaking monastic tradition, twelve jovial friars
gave up their vocation for a questionable existence
on the flying trapeze.

20/25 Point

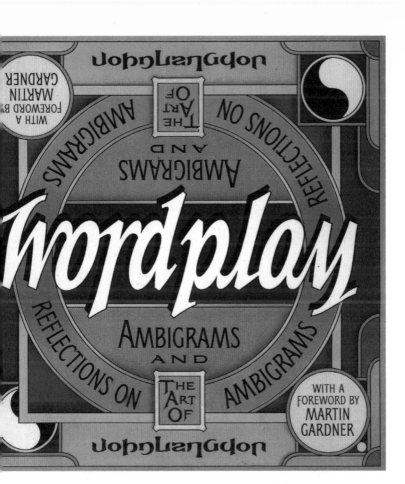

Book cover, John Langdon, 1993

Poster, Sven Quadflieg, 2008

Decorative and Freestyle

Rodrigo Ramírez | tipografia.cl | CD

ABCDEFGH
IJKLMNOPQR
STUVWXYZ
abcdefghijklmn
opqrstuvwxyz
äöüßEt$@?!.,;:*
1234567890

42 Point

_____

Forsaking monastic tradition, twelve
jovial friars gave up their vocation for a
questionable existence on the flying trapeze.

15/25 Point

Decorative and Freestyle

441

ABCDEFGHI
JKLMNOPQR
STUVWXYZ

abcdefghijklmn
opqrstuvwxyz
äöüß&§?!.,:;*
1234567890

32 Point

Forsaking monastic tradition, twelve jovial friars gave up their vocation for a questionable existence on the flying trapeze.

13/25 Point

The Inspired Vegetarian

LOUISE PICKFORD
Photographs by Gus Filgate

Book cover, Lynn Pieroni Fowler, 1993

ABCDEFGH
IJKLMNOPQR
STUVWXYZ
abcdefghijklmn
opqrstuvwxyz
äöüß$%&@?!.,:;*
1234567890

40 Point

Forsaking monastic tradition, twelve jovial
friars gave up their vocation for a questionable
existence on the flying trapeze.

16/25 Point

39 Point

Forsaking monastic tradition, twelve jovial friars gave up their vocation for a questionable existence on the flying trapeze.

15/25 Point

Poster, Till Gathmann, 2004

A B C D E F G H
I J K L M N O P Q R
S T U V W X Y Z
a b c d e f g h i j k l m n
o p q r s t u v w x y z ä ö ü ß
§ & $ @ ? ! . , : *
1 2 3 4 5 6 7 8 9 0

44 Point

Forsaking monastic tradition, twelve jovial friars
gave up their vocation for a questionable existence
on the flying trapeze.

22/25 Point

447

ABCDEFGHIJ

KLMNOPQR

STUVWXYZ

abcdefghijklmn

opqrstuvwxyz

äöüß$%&@?!.,.;*

1234567890

36 Point

Forsaking monastic tradition, twelve jovial friars
gave up their vocation for a questionable existence
on the flying trapeze.

15/25 Point

ABCDEFG
HIJKLMN
OPQRST
UVWXYZ

abcdefghijklmn

opqrstuvwxyzäöü

&%$@?!.,.;*

1234567890

45 Point

Forsaking monastic tradition, twelve
jovial friars gave up their vocation for a
questionable existence on the flying trapeze.

23/25 Point

Decorative and Freestyle

449

ABCDEFGH
IJKLMNOPQ
RSTUVWXYZ
abcdefghijklmn
opqrstuvwxyz
&@?),.;;-
1234567890

55 Point

Forsaking monastic tradition, twelve jovial friars
gave up their vocation for a questionable
existence on the flying trapeze.

22/25 Point

ABCDEFGHIJKLMN

OPQRSTUVWXYZ

abcdefghijklmn

opqrstuvwxyz

äöüß%&?!.,:;*

1234567890

65 Point

Forsaking monastir tradition, tuorlion jovial friars
gawon ŷp tfriir vocation foir a gŷnstionaGln nŷistnirn
on tfn fliĵing trapnzn.

28/25 Point

J&B neat.

J&B Scotch Whisky. Blended and bottled in Scotland by Justerini & Brooks, fine wine and spirit merchants since 1749.
To send a gift of J&B anywhere in the U.S., call 1-800-528-6148. Void where prohibited.

Poster, Roy Grace

60 sekuntia, 2006 | junkohanhero.com | CD

ABCDEFGHIJ
KLMNOPQ
RSTUVWXYZ
ABCDEFGHIJK
LMNOPQRSTU
VWXYZÄÖÜ
$%&@?!..;:*
1234567890

28 Point

FORSAKING MONASTIC TRADITION. TWELVE

JOVIAL FRIARS GAVE UP THEIR VOCATION FOR A

QUESTIONABLE EXISTENCE ON THE FLYING TRAPEZE.

10/25 Point

Decorative and Freestyle

ABCDEFGHIJ
KLMNOPQR
STUVWXYZ
abcdefghijklmn
opqrstuvwxyz
$&@?!.,:;*
1234567890

39 Point

Forsaking monastic tradition, twelve
jovial friars gave up their vocation for a
questionable existence on the flying trapeze.

13/25 Point

Kirk Shelton, 2009 | dafont.com | CD

A B C D E F G H

I J K L M N O P Q

R S T U W X Y Z

a b c d e f g h i j k l m n

o p q r s t u v w x y z

$, & @ ? ! . : ; *

1 2 3 4 5 6 7 8 9 0

36 Point

Forsaking monastic tradition, twelve
jovial friars gave up their vacation for a
questionable existence on the flying trapeze.

14/25 Point

ABCDEFGH

IJKLMNOPQ

RSTUVWXYZ

abcdefghij

klmnopqr

stuvwxyz

1234567890

40 Point

Forsaking monastic tradition,
twelve jovial friars gave up
their vocation for a questionable
existence on the flying trapeze.

13/17 Point

Katharina Putick, 2004 | dakapu.com | CD

ABCDEFGH
IJKLMNOPQ
RSTUVWXYZ
abcdefghijklmn
opqrstuvwxyz
äöüß § &@?![.,:;*
1234567890

32 Point

Forsaking monastic tradition, twelve jovial
friars gave up their vocation for a questionable
existence on the flying trapeze.

10/25 Point

Decorative and Freestyle

457

Poster, Blake Wright, 2009

ABCDEFGHIJ
KLMNOPQR
STUVWXYZ
abcdefghijk
lmnopqrstu
vwxyzäöüß
&@?!.,:;
1234567890

38 Point

Forsaking monastic tradition, twelve jovial

friars gave up their vocation for a questionable

existence on the flying trapeze.

10/25 Point

ABCDEFGH
IJKLMNOPQ
RSTUVWXYZ
abcdefghijk
lmnopqrstu
vwxyzäöüß
&?!.,:;
1234567890

48 Point

Forsaking monastic tradition, twelve

jovial friars gave up their vocation for a

questionable existence on the flying trapeze.

16/25 Point

abcdefghi

ijklmnopq

rstuvwxyz

abcdefghijk

lmnopqrst

uvwxyzäöüß

&%$@?!.,:;·

1234567890

30 Point

forsaking monastic tradition, twelve

jovial friars gave up their vocation for a

questionable existence on the flying trapeze

10/25 Point

Decorative and Freestyle

461

abcdefghijk
lmnopqrstu
uvwxyzäöüß
abcdefghijk
lmnopqrstu
uvwxyzäöüß
$%.&@?!.,.:;   *
1234567890

34 Point

forsaking monastic tradition, twelve
jovial friars gave up their vocation for a
questionable existence on the flying trapeza.

12/25 Point

Decorative and Freestyle

462

Baladi Bar publicity, Ben Wittner, Sascha
Thoma, 2008

ABCDEFGHIJ
KLMNOPQRST
UVWXYZ
abcdefghijklmn
opqrstuvwxyz
xöüß % &@?!.,:;*
1234567890

41 Point

Forsaking monastic tradition, twelve jovial
friars gave up their vocation for a questionable
existence on the flying trapeze.

15/25 Point

464

ABCDEFGHI
JKLMNOPQR
STUVWXYZ

abcdefghijklmn
opqrstuvwxyzäöüß
$%&@?!.,:;*

1234567890

38 Point

Forsaking monastic tradition, twelve jovial
friars gave up their vocation for a questionable
existence on the flying trapeze.

16/25 Point

Gregorius Wisnu, 2008 | dafont.com | CD

ABCDEFGHIJ

KLMNOPQR

STUVWXYZ

abcdefghijklmn

opqrstuvwxyz

$%&@?!.,.;*

1234567890

42 Point

Forsaking monastic tradition, twelve
jovial Friars gave up their vocation For a
questionable existence on the Flying trapeze.

14/25 Point

ABCDEFG
HIIKLMN
OPQRSTU
VWXYZ
&&?¡'"
1234567890

52 Point

FORSAKING MONASTIC TRADITIONS TWELVE

JOVIAL FRIARS GAVE UP THEIR VOCATION FOR A

QUESTIONABLE EXISTENCE ON THE FLYING TRAPEZE.

11/25 Point

$$\mathcal{ABCDEF}$$

$$\mathcal{GHIJK}$$

$$\mathcal{LMNOP}$$

$$\mathcal{QRSTU}$$

$$\mathcal{VWXYZ}$$

62 Point

FORSAKING MONASTIC TRADITION
TWELVE JOVIAL FRIARS GAVE UP
THEIR VOCATION FOR A QUESTIONABLE
EXISTENCE ON THE FLYING TRAPEZE

12/18 Point

Caslon Calligraphic Initials

Paul Lloyd, 2002

moorstation.org | CD

A B C D E

F G H I J

K L M N

O P Q R

S T U V

W X Y Z

38 Point

FORSAKING MONASTIC TRADITION ¶ TWELVE JOVIAL FRIARS GAVE UP THEIR VOCATION FOR A QUESTIONABLE EXISTENCE ON THE FLYING TRAPEZE ¶

7/18 Point

Notes & Contacts

Index of Type Designers

Index of Type Designers

Index of Type Designers

Index of Foundries

Published in 2016 by
Laurence King Publishing Ltd
361–373 City Road
London EC1V 1LR
e-mail: enquiries@laurenceking.com
www.laurenceking.com

ISBN 978-1-78067-758-3

German language edition:
Brush 'n' Script
© (2010 by Verlag Hermann Schmidt
Mainz, Germany www.typografie.de)

Collected and designed
by Geum-Hee Hong with assistance
from Lydia Stockert and Julia Krömer

Pattern design: Geum-Hee Hong
based on an idea by Judith Schalansky

CD-programming: Lydia Stockert

Cover design: Alexandre Coco

Printed in China